How to Build a

Lasting Marriage

How to Build a

Lasting Marriage

Lessons from Bible Couples

by

RUTH AND ELMER L. TOWNS

DESTINY IMAGE® PUBLISHERS, INC.

P.O. Box 310, Shippensburg, PA 17257-0310

"Speaking to the Purposes of God for This Generation and for the Generations to Come."

This book and all other Destiny Image, Revival Press, MercyPlace, Fresh Bread, Destiny Image Fiction, and Treasure House books are available at Christian bookstores and distributors worldwide.

For a U.S. bookstore nearest you, call 1-800-722-6774.

For more information on foreign distributors, call 717-532-3040.

Or reach us on the Internet: www.destinyimage.com.

ISBN 10: 0-7684-3142-5

ISBN 13: 978-0-7684-3142-1

Previous ISBN 0-7852-5022-0 Published in Nashville, Tennessee, by Thomas Nelson, Inc.

Re-release of *Whom God has Joined Together*

For Worldwide Distribution, Printed in the U.S.A.

1 2 3 4 5 6 7 8 9 10 11 / 13 12 11 10 09

Table of Contents

Foreword
Tim and Beverly LaHaye

Tim LaHaye Ministries, El Cajon, California

We have known Elmer and Ruth Towns for more than 30 years of ministry. Elmer, who is a great Bible teacher, has been in our former church in San Diego, California, on many occasions. Ruth is a big supporter of Concerned Women for America, the Washington, DC-based Christian women's pro-family public policy organization that Beverly founded in 1979. Ruth was the adoption caseworker and director of Family Life Services, which is the state-accredited adoption agency of Thomas Road Baptist Church, so Ruth and Beverly have a similar purpose in life to protect the unborn, as well as place unwanted babies in loving Christian homes.

We think it's great that a couple who has served the Lord so faithfully over the years has written a book that will help couples learn the same lessons that Elmer and Ruth have learned. But more than just lessons, Elmer and Ruth's marriage is an example to many couples as they see that they too can serve the Lord together and build a strong Christian home at the same time.

This book is not just Christian advice that comes from their experiences, but, rather, is a strong Bible study that immerses readers into the lives of families in the Bible. The Townses have done an outstanding job of finding the dominant "glue" that holds each Bible couple together and applying that biblical principle to couples today. We can't think of a better way for couples to strengthen their marriages than to study the Scriptures concerning these 12 Bible couples and to apply these practical applications to their own marriage.

There are two things about the book that we particularly enjoy: First, there is a section called Counseling Approach. This is what a counselor might have told these Christian couples as they attempted to live for God. Second, we like the last section of each chapter, Practical Take-Aways. Each chapter ends with these practical projects for each couple to use and strengthen their marriage.

Both of us—Tim and Beverly—have used the written Word to reach other people for Christ, so we know the power of Christian journalism. We believe this book will help couples, and our prayer is that your marriage will be strengthened as you study this book.

Preface
HERE COMES THE BRIDE

*R*ecently, our daughter, Debbie (DJ), married a man who is so closely matched to her that everyone who knows them is amazed.

Roy is a master photographer, having won awards for composition and subject. He is the family head to whom everyone turns when anything broken needs fixing or something new must be made from old parts of machinery or furniture. He is also the one to hold the family together in times of crisis. But that's Debbie, also.

Roy is a historian. He and Debbie reenact historical Virginian events and have taught candle making and bateau navigating on the James River. They attend rendezvous meetings with other reenactors from all over the East Coast. Both love camping and are very "earthy" people. If there is such a thing as a soul mate, Roy and DJ are soul mates.

Because they are unique and totally comfortable with themselves, the wedding plans were unusual. The invitations were printed on brown wrapping paper, the bride's dress was deerskin, their shoes were leather moccasins, and the wedding site was an open field. The reception featured a huge kettle of Brunswick stew and loaves of freshly baked bread. Friends and curious on-lookers gathered around while DJ's brother led the couple in the marriage vows. Dulcimer Dave provided soft music and the couple returned to their campsite on a horse-drawn wagon.

Wedding plans sometimes take months and are usually the culmination of a girl's lifelong dreams. The preparation is exciting, and everything must be exactly right.

I (Ruth) remember my wedding. I'm sure I must have tried on every dress in the bridal shop. Even the undergarments were chosen with utmost care. I worried about what shoes to wear because, back then, Elmer was shorter than I was. I was picky about the flowers, cake, invitations, and the rings. I wanted all my friends there, so we spent hours finding addresses for people we had not seen for a long time. The honeymoon plans were discussed and changed several times, and every detail of who rode in which car and which car was the getaway car was part of the carefully decided details.

After all, we planned to spend the rest of our lives together.

I am planning to spend eternity with my heavenly Bridegroom. Sometimes I wonder how much preparation and planning I am doing and how excited I get as I look toward that time.

He will provide the dress—a robe of righteousness. I don't have to be concerned about where I'll live because He is building a mansion for me. He is doing His part, but I'm a little slow on my end of it.

I know I need to spend more time getting to know Him. Elmer wrote me love letters that I still have. God has written love letters to me, too, but sometimes I can't find time to read them.

Elmer and I talked every chance we got before we got married, but sometimes I seem to rush the intimate talks with my heavenly Bridegroom.

I talked about Elmer all the time—to everyone. I was not embarrassed to talk about him, even to complete strangers. Isn't it amazing that I sometimes find it difficult to talk about the Lord with the same freedom and love?

Elmer and I enjoy doing things for each other. I know him so well that I can usually guess where he wants to go out to eat. But I can still pick out a tie to surprise him now and then. Sometimes we even complete a sentence for each other. I want to know the Lord like that! I need to know what pleases Him and that He takes pleasure in what I do.

It's all about preparation, getting to know the other person better than anyone else. Like the song: "Getting to know you, getting to know all about you, getting to know all the beautiful and new things I'm learning about you, day by day."

The wedding march is about to begin! Here comes the bride.

Chapter 1

Isaac and Rebekah
LEARNING COMMUNICATION

Introduction by David Yonggi and Grace Kim-Cho The Yoido Full Gospel Church, Seoul, Korea

Years ago, we had breakfast in Seoul, Korea, with Elmer Towns. This was not the first time we had met Elmer or eaten together. We have been friends for more than 25 years, and we love and respect one another. Our unique bond is fasting and prayer and our love for the Lord's Prayer. In particular, we have both written on these topics. We consider it a privilege to write the introduction to this chapter on Isaac and Rebekah.

Isaac was a godly young man, the child of Abraham, and a spiritual father. He was the product of a supernatural birth, and God had promised to send Jesus Christ through Isaac. Therefore, it was imperative for him to marry "in the Lord" and to be faithful to the Lord all his life.

God supernaturally brought Rebekah into Isaac's life. Theirs is a beautiful love story. We have seen the same love story acted out in many couples in our church, The Yoido Full Gospel Church, in Seoul, Korea.

Isaac and Rebekah had difficulties adjusting and relating to one another. Elmer and Ruth Towns poignantly tell the story of how Isaac wouldn't talk to his wife and how she constantly ran ahead of God's will. As a result, there were several occasions of a broken relationship in the home. Again, we have seen the same thing happen in couples in our church. Just as the answer in Bible times was being correctly related to God, so is it today.

We pray that many couples will read this book and begin to talk together—thus strengthening the marriage God has given them. May God use this book to strengthen Christian marriages around the world.

Learning Communication

Genesis 24–29

A wedding is one of the most wonderful events in life. It lifts our spirits and gives us hope for the future. Why? While the bride is the most beautiful she's ever been in her life and the ceremony and expensive reception that follow are lovely, a wedding is beautiful because it is a promise of perfect harmony between two people.

The wedding of Isaac and Rebekah was one of the most special marriages in the Bible. Isaac was the son of a powerful man, and what girl wouldn't have wanted to marry Abraham's son? Isaac would inherit his father's wealth, and his children would be in the lineage to the Messiah. Rebekah was beautiful, youthful, energetic, and from the right family. She bubbled with enthusiasm and lived life to the fullest. This "perfect" marriage that began so wonderfully...slowly eroded.

Their problem wasn't money, position, or physical impairment. They had all the ingredients for a perfect marriage—except one. They didn't communicate.

Tender Beginnings

Abraham, the patriarch, was old and knew he would die soon. He knew his son needed a wife, and he couldn't travel back to his home to choose the girl. Abraham called on his wise servant, Eliezer, and said, *"...you will not take a wife for my son from the daughters of the Canaanites, among whom I dwell; but you shall go to my country and to my family, and take a wife for my son Isaac"* (Gen. 24:3-4). Abraham thus established a set of parameters in choosing a mate for his son.

First, moral character is important.

The Canaanites who surrounded Abraham were immoral people; therefore, a Canaanite woman was the wrong choice for his son.

Second, believers should marry believers.

Abraham drew from the principle seen throughout Scripture that when a believer marries an ungodly person, the latter is sanctified through their faithful spouse (see 1 Cor. 7:10-16).

Counseling Approach

Eliezer was a trusted servant and a great counselor. He had all the answers for Rebekah's questions. But should he have told her about Isaac and left nothing for her to discover on her own?

He chose a bouncy, energetic workaholic for a quiet, thoughtful, rich kid. Neither Rebekah nor Isaac had any idea how their differences would complement each other or complicate their lives.

Studying the differences in other people will help you understand yourself. Open and frank communication is necessary, or a couple can drift apart. Like Isaac, a man might wrap himself in his quiet world of meditation. Like Rebekah, a woman may energetically venture out on her own to find the satisfaction in life that she seeks.

What does Second Corinthians 6:14-15 say about the importance of marrying a believer?

_____

_____

_____

_____

Third, pray and always seek God's guidance.

As Eliezer traveled from the Holy Land back to Abraham's people to find a wife for Isaac, he prayed.

In Genesis 24:12, what was Eliezer's prayer as he began his journey?

_____

_____

_____

_____

When Eliezer met Rebekah and asked for water, *"She said, 'Drink, my lord.' Then she quickly let her pitcher down to her hand, and gave him a drink"* (Gen. 24:18). Rebekah was a diligent and hard worker who also offered water to Eliezer's camels. (This probably involved more than 100 gallons of water.)

Genesis 24:16 describes Rebekah as having two very desirable qualities. What qualities did Rebekah bring into this marriage?

_____

_____

_____

_____

So who should pray? Parents should begin praying for their children's mate long before the children are born, and should continue praying up until the time of marriage. But both the

> man and woman should also pray for a long time concerning their mate. My mother taught me to pray for the man I would marry along with the "Now I Lay Me Down" prayer. "God bless Mommy, Daddy, David (my brother), and the man I marry."

Rebekah was the kind of girl who bounced into a room, met everyone, and became the center of attention. She was energetic, friendly, and outgoing. A wonderful quality for a wife is that she puts the needs of others first. Not only did Rebekah meet others well, she understood their needs and offered help. She even invited them to her home. But beyond all that, Rebekah could make a firm decision and make it stick. As her family was debating whether she should go immediately to Isaac, she said, *"I will go"* (Gen. 24:58).

What qualities are necessary for a woman to be a good wife?
Look in Titus 2:4 and Proverbs 31:10-31.

_____

_____

_____

_____

_____

"God bless Mommy, Daddy, David (my brother) and the man I marry."

What Qualities Did Isaac Bring into the Marriage?

Their Primary Obstacle: Lack of Children

When we first see Isaac in this story, he is out in the fields praying. He was a quiet, nonconfrontational, meditative man. Isaac inherited money from his father, along with servants and possessions. More to the point, he inherited his father's title and lineage. But most importantly, Isaac lived with a sense of God's divine purpose in his life (see Gen. 26:24-29).

What qualities are necessary for a man to be a good husband? Look in Ephesians 5:25-33 and First Peter 3:7.

_____

_____

_____

_____

How Can This Marriage Be Described?

This is a marriage of opposites. Sometimes opposites attract to make a good marriage. They learn from each other, help each other, and both grow in the Lord. But opposites can also repel. They can end up fighting. Two equals (two people of the same nature) can have a good marriage because they think alike, dream alike, and act alike. However, two equals may not challenge each other, and they may not grow individually. Two equals can become too comfortable, and while there is nothing wrong with comfort when you have to go to sleep, a marriage takes work, sweat, and commitment.

What Were the Positive Aspects of Isaac and Rebekah's Relationship?

When Rebekah first met her husband, *"she took a veil and covered herself"* (Gen. 24:65). While this doesn't mean much today, it was the custom in Bible times and indicated a respected social expectation in their culture.

They were also respectful of their families. Before Rebekah left, she got her family's blessing, and then she became part of Isaac's family.

According to Genesis 24:67, what did Isaac do next?

_____

_____

_____

_____

Women may see things in other women that men may not see, so it is not unusual for a man to listen to the insight of his mother about his future wife.

According to Ephesians 5:28, how should a husband treat his wife?
And why is that important?

_____

_____

_____

_____

_____

Love is the important foundation of a marriage. Speaking of Isaac and Rebekah, the Bible says, *"he loved her"* (Gen. 24:67). A marriage without love is just a social contract that some feel they can break when they feel they no longer love one another. But marriage is a union where the two become one. The two are commanded to love one another. They must build their love to endure storms and trials.

And they were tender toward one another.

A few years after the marriage, Isaac and Rebekah found themselves in Philistine territory. They were living among the heathen, but even then the Bible describes Isaac as *"showing endearment to Rebekah his wife"* (Gen. 26:8).

According to First Peter 3:3-4, what should be the most attractive thing about a wife?

_____

_____

_____

_____

_____

_____

Three Observations About Marital Strife and Children

1. Children can't solve a problem.

2. Sometimes children can accentuate the problem.

3. Sometimes children can bring a couple together.

Their Primary Obstacle: Lack of Children

There was heartbreak in this marriage because Rebekah was not able to have children. The lack of a child was a major problem for Isaac. Today when a couple is squabbling and talking about a divorce, some might mistakenly counsel, "If you have a baby, it will keep you together." While a baby may keep you together for a while, that is certainly not the reason to have a baby.

What Compounded Their Problem?

First, we see a young girl with a lively personality who can't have a baby. Today, infertility is a very real problem, and it certainly shouldn't reflect badly on either the husband or the wife. But in Bible times, barrenness was a great embarrassment to a woman. If a woman couldn't have a child, it was believed to be because of sin in her life or some physical problem that made her less of a woman.

Remember, Isaac was the meditative one, so what did he do? He prayed on behalf of his wife to the Lord, and *"The Lord granted his plea, and Rebekah his wife conceived"* (Gen. 25:21).

Aside from a lot of prayer, Isaac probably didn't talk about much at all. Rebekah's vivacious personality probably motivated her to talk about everything, and Isaac's retiring ways may have led to the communication problems. Regardless of how it started, things became difficult in their relationship when Rebekah began having problems with her pregnancy.

What Were the Results of Her Difficult Pregnancy?

Whether it was physical discomfort or real pain, what does Genesis 25:22 say about Rebekah's pregnancy?

_____

_____

_____

_____

_____

Isaac apparently didn't talk about this problem with his wife, and since Rebekah couldn't communicate with her husband, the Bible says, *"she went to inquire of the*

Lord" (Gen. 25:22). Although it is good for a wife to pray when she and her husband are having difficulties, it is better when the two of them talk and pray together.

How Can Couples Build Better Communication?

First, give each other an opportunity to talk, and don't push your mate when he or she is not ready.

Second, find times when your mate is most open to communication and make the most of that opportunity. Sometimes we wonder why our spouse seems disinterested in what we have to say. The truth is, we didn't get his or her attention in the first place.

Third, don't judge your spouse. Sometimes we are quick to correct what our spouse says, or we disagree with him or her. This can shut down conversation.

Fourth, it's OK to disagree, but be kind and respectful to one another. Don't use sarcasm.

Fifth, we all want to be understood by our mate, and we often complain when that doesn't happen. If we would only try to understand our spouse, he or she might, in turn, try to understand us.

Sixth, don't jump to conclusions. Be patient and listen.

And finally, try to give your undivided attention when your spouse wants to share something with you. Sometimes we can give the impression that whatever our spouse says isn't important. We need to put other things aside and communicate.

Using Children to Fulfill a Need

Here was a marriage where two people were opposites; she was vivacious and outgoing and he was quiet and contemplative. To compound the problem, the couple played favorites with their children. Isaac was partial to Esau, the oldest son, and Rebekah was partial to her baby, Jacob. Isaac might have been partial to Esau because he was a rugged outdoorsman who loved to go hunting and kill wild game. Jacob, on the other hand, learned the culinary arts and could run errands for his mother. We see Isaac's vicarious pride in the manly ways of his son, Esau, while we see Rebekah enjoying the companionship of her son, Jacob. This biblical family is a reflection of some contemporary families. Scripture reminds us that there is nothing new under the sun. That covers family issues, too!

Where Did It Start?

When you look back at Isaac's parents, Abraham and Sarah, you find a husband and wife who quarreled over their children. When Isaac was a small baby, Abraham and Sarah got into a big argument over Isaac and Ishmael. Ishmael was Isaac's son, but Sarah was not his mother. Ishmael lived in the family with his mother, Hagar. Even though this seems to be an unnatural relationship to us today, in Bible times, a man could have a child by one of his slaves. Since Sarah appeared unable to conceive, Abraham had a child with his slave, Hagar. The story of this difficult arrangement ended when Sarah demanded that Abraham get rid of Hagar and her son, Ishmael. Ironically, a generation later, Isaac and Rebekah fought over their children.

In Genesis 25:28, what is said about Isaac and Rebekah's relationship with their children?

_____

_____

_____

_____

What Happens to Children When Their Parents Take Sides?

Parental favoritism can upset a child's personality. Rebekah made sure Jacob had the best of everything. So some time later, Rebekah devised a plan to make sure Jacob received the spiritual blessing from his father. At the same time, Isaac saw

Esau as the extension of his dream.

Children bond with their parents to the same degree that parents bond with each other. When parents fight, children are frightened and become insecure about the family unit.

Jacob rebelled against his parents by stealing the birthright, and later the blessing, from his brother, Esau. God had told Rebekah, *"And the older shall serve the younger"* (Gen. 25:23). If Rebekah had told Isaac and both parents had talked to their children, Jacob wouldn't have had to steal anything. But the lack of communication was the problem.

In Genesis 27:36, what is Esau's reaction to losing everything to his younger brother?

_____

_____

_____

_____

In retaliation, Esau ran away and married two Hittite women. After the birthright was stolen by Jacob, it would have been the perfect time to have a "family council" to talk over problems and make long-term plans. But when parents refuse to face their problems, the problems just get bigger.

Isaac had secretly planned to bless Esau (Gen. 27:1-4) and give him the majority of the financial inheritance. Perhaps Isaac wouldn't have made secret plans to bless Esau if Rebekah had told him about Jacob being God's choice. But their marriage lacked the critical element of communication. So Rebekah sprang into action and devised the plan for Jacob to get the blessing rather than Esau (see Gen. 27:15-17).

Let the words of my mouth and the meditations of my heart be acceptable in Your sight, O Lord, my strength and my Redeemer (Psalm 19:14).

Isaac unknowingly blessed his son, Jacob, promising that Jacob would be the spiritual head of the family and the one through whom the Messiah would come. When Esau arrived at his father's tent to get the blessing from him, Isaac trembled. He would not and could not reverse himself. The blessing was an irreversible verbal oath. Even in this emotionally tense moment, Isaac's word was his bond.

As a result of this treachery, Esau hated Jacob and vowed to kill him (see Gen. 27:41). This would have been a perfect time for father and mother to repair all the damage that had been done over the years. But it was too late—the damage had been done. Isaac wouldn't talk and Rebekah wouldn't listen. Again, Rebekah covered up the real problem by telling her husband a half-truth. She complained about Esau's choice of a wife under the guise of her plan to send Jacob to her people to find a wife. How else could she keep Jacob safe from the wrath of Esau?

So what has happened? Rebekah has alienated her husband, she has estranged her firstborn son, and now she has sent Jacob away to keep him from harm's way. Unfortunately, she died before Jacob returned, and she never saw her beloved son again.

After reading Ephesians 5:22-33, in your own words, describe what you think the source of happiness in a good marriage should be.

_____

_____

_____

_____

_____

Practical Take-Aways

It takes two to communicate and two to quarrel.

These are the greatest lessons to learn from Rebekah and Isaac. While she might have thought her husband was at fault because of his contemplative separation, Isaac might have blamed Rebekah for their problems. But both were equally responsible for their problems and lack of communication.

It doesn't really matter who is at fault.

When couples realize they are in trouble, they should remember their marital promise. When you make the marital promise to each other, the Lord says you are one. When you realize you're becoming two, going in two different directions, and you have two opinions, STOP! Call a time-out so both of you can come together as one and talk about the problem.

Remember the power of two.

Come together and say, "I need you," and then say, "We need God." You can't build a marital home on one person; it takes the power of two and the power of prayer. Both a good husband and a good wife are needed for a good marriage, to train good children and to plan for a good future.

Begin sharing ideas and dreams.

If it's your nature to be quiet, try to talk. If you've been critical, begin to listen. Talk about the future. It's where both of you and your children will live. Be careful to plant healthy ideas in your children and dream reachable goals for yourselves. Let your children see you praying, and pray together as a family.

Approach your problems as one person.

Make a list of the obstacles that the two of you have. Each of you should suggest issues that have come between you. When you get the obstacles down on paper, try to prioritize them from the biggest issue down to the most minor issue. There should be one list completed together as a couple—and a different one from your individual lists. As you talk and pray about your mutual problems, God can give you answers.

Journaling

Writing your thoughts is a discipline that makes you think clearly about a subject. Since you are serious about developing a strong marriage, use the following questions to guide your thoughts and writings. Remember, writing will clarify your thinking when you write the things you plan to do.

For example:

Lord, as we look at Rebekah and Isaac, we are so sorry for times when we've allowed our own selfishness and jealousy to overtake our thoughts and our decisions. We're sorry for the times we excluded each other from those thoughts and decisions. Please forgive us. Let our marriage be an example to our children, not a force that drives them away. Thank You for guiding our love for each other.

1. Recall some occasions where you've had great communication in the past. Why was it wonderful?

His Response

Her Response

_____   _____

_____   _____

_____   _____

_____   _____

_____   _____

_____   _____

_____   _____

_____   _____

_____   _____

2. What are some external factors that block communication between
   you and your mate?

His Response   *Her Response*

_____   _____

_____   _____

_____   _____

_____   _____

_____   _____

_____   _____

_____   _____

3. What will you do differently to more aggressively communicate with
   your mate this week?

His Response   *Her Response*

_____   _____

_____   _____

_____   _____

_____   _____

_____   _____

_____   _____

_____   _____

_____   _____

4. What are some of your traits that make for great communication? Poor communication?

His Response   *Her Response*

_____   _____

_____   _____

_____   _____

_____   _____

_____   _____

_____   _____

Marriage-Strengthening Exercises

Go on a date.

Go out for a meal (without the kids) so the two of you can talk. If needed, prepare a list of things you can discuss.

Go on a second honeymoon.

Go on a second honeymoon to the place where you originally felt great happiness and joy, or go to some other place that has great meaning for both of you.

Practice talking.

Practice talking through your needs or complaints. You can't expect your mate to know your mind if you don't communicate.

Observe and discuss.

Observe couples you admire. Discuss why you admire them.

Listen.

God gave us two ears and one mouth so that we may hear twice as much as we speak!

Chapter 2

Jacob and Rachel
LEARNING CONTENTMENT

Introduction by Mike and Cindy Jacobs
Generals of Intercession, Colorado Springs, Colorado

Marriage is one of life's greatest adventures! At the time of this writing, we have been married for 29 years. The other day, we shared a moment of "down time" and thought about the fact that we have been married longer than we were single. In fact, those single days almost seem like they were other people rather than us. Come to think of it, we *were* other people.

One key to married life is realizing that you have made a commitment and covenant before God. This brings a depth of contentment that one might not otherwise attain. We know that, despite a few extra pounds and a few suspicious-looking gray hairs, we aren't looking for anyone else to fulfill us.

In thinking of a future spouse, realize that the covenant decision that you make is critical to the success of the marriage. Part of that covenant is the choice to be transparent with one another and not hide secrets. In the following chapter, Rachel was deceitful in her ways. And Jacob was also a deceiver. However, we know that God transformed him.

When considering a marriage partner, look for character qualities that will last even if the clothing size increases. A person who is godly will have eyes only for you and no one else. They will not have anything at all to hide and will also show constancy in their ways.

We love each other very much today. Our love is richer in many ways, even though we have had our challenging moments. Look into the life of the person you are considering to marry before you leap. Measure his or her character by God's Word. Then you will find that your days together will grow increasingly more precious with each passing year.

Learning Contentment

Genesis 28–32

Jacob was a young, unmarried man when his brother, Esau, threatened to kill him and he was forced to run away from home. Jacob had tricked his brother out of the birthright to become the spiritual head of the family and to receive a double portion of inheritance. Jacob's mother sent him back to Mesopotamia—the land between the Tigris and Euphrates Rivers—to live with her brother, Laban, until things settled down at home.

When Jacob left his home for a new life, little did he know that he would never see his mother again. The first night on the road, the Lord said to him, *"Behold, I am with you and will keep you wherever you go, then I will bring you back to this Promised Land, for I will not leave you until I have finished everything I have promised you"* (Gen. 28:15, author's translation).

When Jacob neared Haran, the land of his mother's family, he saw shepherds sitting around a well. He asked, "Do you know Laban, the son of Nahor?"

Counseling Approach

Siblings fight. Did you ever see children in a family who didn't fight? A younger child sees the older one get new clothes while he or she gets the hand-me-downs. Big brothers and sisters can become increasingly insensitive to their younger siblings as their own social world expands.

Sometimes parents unintentionally favor the cute "baby of the family" with softer discipline and even spoil him or her. Parents will plant seeds of habit in their children that, good or bad, will govern their behavior the rest of their lives.

> Not only would Rachel's older sister, Leah, marry Jacob first, but Leah would have children first. Rachel knew she had Jacob's love, but she couldn't seem to have his children. She would be disgraced and embarrassed.
>
> Sibling rivalry became pure jealousy and grew into marital dysfunction. Be careful—your children will be influenced by your attitudes and actions. Parents teach good and bad behavior when they don't realize they're being observed.

"Yes," a young man answered. Then, pointing to a beautiful young lady coming down the road, he explained, *"His daughter Rachel is coming with the sheep"* (Gen. 29:4-6). The young men were assigned to take care of the well, but Jacob convinced them to go about their duties because he would take care of the well. When he saw Rachel, it was love at first sight. She *"was beautiful of form and appearance"* (Gen. 29:17). Since young boys like to show off to impress young girls, he quickly rolled the stone from the well and watered all of Laban's sheep.

Because he was passionate, *"Jacob kissed Rachel, and lifted up his voice and wept"* (Gen. 29:11). He knew God had guided him on this journey, and now he felt Rachel was the answer to his prayer. While our culture might frown on men who express their feelings so readily, Jacob wept at the providential care and guidance of God.

What is the wrong motive for marriage? Read Romans 8:5-6
and Second Corinthians 10:7.

_____

_____

_____

_____

_____

"Yes," a young
man answered.

How Long Before Engagement?

• Long enough to know the character he or she brings to a lifelong commitment.

• Long enough to know if it's true love and not just sexual attraction.

• Long enough to know the real person and not just an idealized dream of the other person.

True Love Flourishes with Unvarnished Truth

Jacob stayed with Uncle Laban for about a month. Jacob probably spent too much time talking to his daughter, Rachel, instead of earning his keep in Laban's fields. Since young Jacob didn't have a dowry to offer for the marriage of Rachel, Laban suggested a plan. He said, "If you work for me, I'll give you my daughter as a bride."

Jacob stayed with Uncle Laban for about a month.

"I will serve you seven years for Rachel your younger daughter," young Jacob proposed to Laban (Gen. 29:18). While it was not a hasty marriage, it surely was a hasty decision. Jacob was about to be tricked. What did Jacob know about Rachel, other than her outward beauty? How long should a man know a woman before proposing?

What advice could be given to a young man thinking about marriage?
See Proverbs 18:22.

_____

_____

_____

_____

_____

According to Titus 2:4-5, what advice could be given to a young woman thinking about marriage?

_____

_____

_____

_____

_____

Can a Marriage Begin With Physical Attraction and Grow Into Lasting Love?

This relationship of Jacob and Rachel began with mere attraction. However, Rachel and Jacob would be separated during the seven years of servitude. Jacob would be keeping sheep in the fields; Rachel would be near the house under the watchful eye of her mother.

Did Jacob Lose His Feelings for Rachel During the Seven Years of Service?

It seems that absence made his heart grow fonder. *"So Jacob served seven years for Rachel, and they seemed only a few days to him because of the love he had for her"* (Gen. 29:20).

Marry in Haste, Repent in Leisure.

- Infatuation is always in a hurry, because it is self–centered.

- Infatuation says I must marry soon, because you make me feel great, and I want more.

- Love says, "*I can wait to make sure that marriage is good for us.*"

When the seven years of service were over, Jacob quickly asked for Rachel and the marriage banquet. He felt getting Rachel would solve all his problems and they would live happily ever after. But the devious Laban substituted Leah for Rachel in the tent on the wedding night. Later, he would tell Jacob, "I can't give my younger daughter before the older." But all the while, Laban was scheming against the young Jacob, who was leading with his heart. Jacob the trickster was tricked by the sly Laban.

When the seven years of service were over, Jacob quickly asked for Rachel and the marriage banquet.

A marriage can have no depth when it is solemnized by trickery or through mere inducements like sex, money, the good life, or even children. Marriage is not one big date. Many have made an empty promise that they didn't intend to keep because they wanted to get married. Men sometimes promise they will quit drinking or running around with the boys or give up certain habits—"If only you'll marry me."

What Was Laban's Solution to the Problem?

When Jacob finished letting off steam about being deceived, Laban explained to him that he had another plan. *"Fulfill her week, and we will give you this one also for the service which you will serve with me still another seven years"* (Gen. 29:27).

All Jacob had to do was give Leah one happy week of marriage, then the family would permit Rachel to marry Jacob—after seven more years of work. Many commentators think that Jacob could have rejected Leah and not married her. After all, Jacob did agree on a "contract" for the younger daughter, Rachel. Maybe Jacob married Leah because he was concerned about losing his down payment, the seven years of service. If he turned Leah down, he'd walk away with nothing.

> *It is more likely to be true love if it endures the first separation.*

Other commentators say that Jacob accepted Leah as his wife simply because it was God's will. While Leah was not as beautiful, nor was she Jacob's choice, it seems that Leah was God's choice. Jesus, the Messiah, came through Leah. Also, when Jacob died, he chose to be buried next to Leah, who had borne him ten sons. Perhaps Jacob should have walked away with Leah and forgotten Rachel. But he was listening to his heart, not his head. There are many men like Jacob who haven't let go of an infatuation with someone very beautiful in the past. Anyone can become addicted to the pleasant memories of a lost love and rob them of happiness in a healthy marriage. They only remember the illusion of the past that never really existed—the unattainable ideal.

Does God's Will Include Bigamy?

The answer obviously is "NO!" God's plan from the beginning has always been one man for one woman, for one lifetime. However, when you see Jacob with two wives, and the blessings of God upon his life, what does that tell you about God working out His plan? First of all, God uses people where He finds them, and He uses their sinful lives for His purposes. People are fallen human beings—none of us are sinless. God purposely uses imperfect people to carry out His perfect plan to reveal His glory. Jacob chose two wives. Even though God blessed Jacob in a bigamous marriage, he had twice the problems, twice the heartache, and twice the deception to deal with.

Lessons My Mother Taught Me

Never marry a man to change him.

Never marry on promises to reform.

So Why Include the Story of a Bigamist in the Bible?

The story of two wives had to be included because that's the way it happened. The Bible describes, as well as prescribes.

What is the difference between a good man and woman and a foolish man and woman? Read Proverbs 12:2-4 for the answer.

_____

_____

_____

_____

_____   *So Why Include the*

_____   *Story of a Bigamist in*

_____   *the Bible?*

_____

_____

What Was Unjustified About Rachel's Jealousy?

- Rachel had the gift of beauty.

- Rachel had her husband's love.

- Rachel had everything in life except children.

What Was Rachel's Response When Leah Had Children?

Rachel developed a cancerous jealousy of Leah. She went to her husband to complain, *"Give me children, or else I die!"* (Gen. 30:1). Rachel's immaturity here may reveal a somewhat spoiled childhood as the younger sibling. She always got her way.

When Rachel fussed at Jacob, he fussed back: *"Am I in the place of God, who has withheld from you the fruit of the womb?"* (Gen. 30:2). The sweet, little girl was becoming envious, demanding, and discontented. People can't be made happy by giving them everything they want.

Today we see the sad irony of discontented couples who desperately want children alongside others who reject the unborn child they have. The problem is not the outward circumstances; it's a heart problem. There are bored homemakers who want to go to work while there are working mothers longing to stay home with their children. There are people who don't like their homes, their jobs, the amount of money their spouse makes, their spouse's habits, or even their spouse. Life is made up of choices. People choose the bad attitudes they express. Just as you can change your choice, so an attitude can be chosen.

Discontentment: A Downward Spiral

- Discontentment turns love into disillusionment.

- Discontentment turns love into resentment.

- Discontentment turns love into hatred and rejection.

Dealing With Discontentment

- Talk it out together honestly, patiently, and lovingly.

- Change your expectations—make them realistic, but encouraging.

- Talk about the reasons for your discontentment without accusing.

- Focus on your spouse's good qualities and spiritual gifts.

- Don't feed your discontentment—*"Godliness with contentment is great gain"* (1 Tim. 6:6).

- Reeducate your desires—*"I have learned in whatever state I am, to be content"* (Phil. 4:11).

How Did Rachel Deal with Her Childlessness?

For a girl who had such advantages, Rachel wasn't content without a baby. Her older sister was now more celebrated than her, having one baby after another. So Rachel devised a plan. "Rachel told Jacob, *'Sleep with my servant, Bilhah, and she shall bear children for you'"* (Gen. 30:3, author's translation). Rachel was determined to have a child, even if it was by her servant girl.

How Did Rachel Get Along with Her Sister in the Home?

Obviously, Rachel was the dominant presence. Most likely, she always got her way because of two things: First, she had Jacob's love, and second, she had a dominating vengeance. Rachel boasted, *"With many wrestlings I have wrestled with my sister, and I have indeed won"* (Gen. 30:8, author's translation).

But just having children with her maidservant didn't satisfy Rachel. She always wanted something she didn't have. She wanted her own child. Leah's four-year-old boy, Reuben, found some special roots called mandrakes (something like rhubarb) and brought them home to Leah. According to the tradition of their day, mandrakes would make one fertile. Rachel saw them in the tent and begged for them. Leah angrily replied, *"Is it a small matter that you have taken away my husband? Would you take away my son's mandrakes also?"* (Gen. 30:15).

These two sisters spit out their jealousy and venom at each other, but selfish Rachel wanted the special roots more than anything else in life; even more than the love of her husband. She promised to get Jacob to sleep with Leah that night if she would give her the roots (see Gen. 30:15).

Read Proverbs 9:13 and 21:19. In what ways does Rachel fit these verses?

_____

_____

_____

_____

_____

Because Leah was always in second place, she would do anything to receive love from Jacob. She gave Rachel the roots and accepted Rachel's promise. That night, Jacob indeed came to Leah and, in God's providence, Leah again conceived and delivered another son.

Was Rachel Content When She Finally Gave Birth to a Son?

After years of praying and waiting, God finally blessed her. We don't have any idea if the mandrake roots had anything to do with it, but she did conceive, and the pregnancy went to its full term. Rachel delivered a boy, the eleventh son of Jacob. The new baby was called Joseph, which means, "May he add." Even in the name Rachel gave her son, she again reveals her lack of contentment when she said, *"The Lord shall add to me another son"* (Gen. 30:24).

Because of her discontented heart, Rachel was never satisfied. She wasn't happy with one son; she wanted another. When she counted her rival's many sons compared to her one son, she still felt empty and jealous. Every time she saw little Joseph running around the tent, it reminded her of her hunger to have another son. Rachel was not going to let her younger glory be overshadowed by her sister, Leah.

How Did Rachel Show Her Nature When Leaving Her Father's Family?

The time came for Jacob to leave his father-in-law, Laban. He had worked hard for Laban, all the while becoming richer while Laban became poorer. After Jacob worked for 14 years for his two wives, he continued working for Laban to support his growing family. Jacob gathered herds of his own. Even though Laban and Jacob agreed on the amount of Jacob's wages at the beginning of each year, God blessed Jacob more than Laban. Jacob was getting rich. While the situation seemed acceptable to both men, it was not acceptable to Laban's sons. They constantly criticized Jacob to their father.

Jacob felt their snipping was unjust and knew he had to leave Mesopotamia to return home to the future Holy Land. But he couldn't risk leaving in the daylight, so he waited until Laban went off to shear his sheep. Quickly Jacob packed up his 11 sons, 2 wives, and all his possessions and began the long journey. Just before leaving, Rachel stole her father's valuable idols (Gen. 31:19). This doesn't mean Rachel was an idolater or that she would have worshiped idols. The images represented the family's inheritance, and the child that possessed the idols was supposed to inherit. Again, Rachel was up to her old tricks. She stole the idols before they left to try to assure something from Laban's estate despite leaving.

Laban and his men pursued Jacob on horses, while Jacob and his family traveled slowly, herding the flocks along with them. When Laban caught up with them, he and his warriors began rummaging through all the baggage to find his idols. Jacob claimed innocence—he knew he didn't steal the idols and didn't think anyone else had them.

When Laban came to Rachel sitting on the camel, she claimed it was her menstrual time of the month and wouldn't dismount from the camel. In reality, she was sitting on the idols. Rachel was beautiful, but she was also very shallow and devious.

Did They Live Happily Ever After?

Despite Rachel's shenanigans, Jacob still protected her more than the rest of the family when they faced danger (Gen. 33:2). Jacob's heart was shackled to Rachel's allure over him.

Rachel had said early in life, "Give me a son, or I die!" She didn't know that in having her second son she would die. Sometimes the self-centered pursuit of our heart's desire can result in great loss, pain, and even destruction. Rachel had severe labor pains when giving birth to her second son, which some have said caused her death. Right before she died, she named her second son Ben-Oni, which means, "Son of My Sorrow." Jacob, however, renamed him Benjamin, meaning "Son of My Right Hand."

Read Proverbs 11:29. What does this verse say about the result of Rachel's actions?

_____

_____

_____

_____

_____

Jacob buried Rachel by the side of the road where a tomb still remains today between Bethlehem and Jerusalem. We have visited Rachel's tomb frequently and each time have thought about the strange relationships in this dysfunctional family. There she is buried alone. Jacob is buried by the side of Leah, miles away in Hebron.

Did Jacob Ever Get over Rachel After She Died?

Even though Jacob had 12 sons, he was overprotective of Benjamin because he reminded him of Rachel, the wife he loved the most. Jacob never broke free of her tender shackles, even after she was dead.

What Can Be Said About the Burial of the Two Wives?

It's ironic that the relationship you see in the burial of the two wives never happens in real life. Jacob requested to be buried by the side of Leah (Gen. 49:29-33), and this was done. Leah, despite never being able to enjoy Jacob's side in life, rested there in death. At the same time, this left discontented Rachel, who had everything, lying alone by the side of the road.

Notice the context of marriage in Hebrews 13:4-5. What should be one's objective in marriage?

_____

_____

_____

_____

Is discontentment poisoning your marriage?

You can assess your level of satisfaction to determine if you are capable of being a happy person. Are you happy with your spouse? With your home? With yourself? If you aren't satisfied with your marriage, you're taking something away from all of them. Is something vital really wrong or is your heart somewhat like Rachel's?

Is your discontentment keeping you from enjoying life?

If you are always seeking happiness somewhere else, with someone else, or doing something else, then you're not happy at home. Since home is a large part of our identity and the place we spend most of our lives, then discontentment with the home (house, marriage, spouse, etc.) produces discontentment with life.

Does your discontentment keep you from relating to people?

If you are discontented, you're not happy with the people around you. A discontented person always wants more: more money, more fun, more adventure. Usually, a discontented person doesn't help another person find happiness in life. A chronically discontented person like Rachel is only concerned with making himself or herself happy. Discontentment is the fruit of selfishness.

Discontentment leads to loneliness.

Discontentment will cut you off from those who can bring happiness. When you're discontented with life, you search in every direction to find a shallow satisfaction. Deep joy, however, can be had by a quiet, unselfish heart.

Your first and greatest contentment is found in God.

This chapter doesn't focus on the deeper Christian life; but remember who made you to know His joy and not to see it first in things, money, advancement, or even in other people. *"Be content with such things as you have. For He Himself has said, 'I will never leave you nor forsake you'"* (Heb.13:5).

Journaling

Writing your thoughts is a discipline that makes you think clearly about a subject. Since you are serious about developing a strong marriage, use the following questions to guide your thoughts and writings. Remember, writing will clarify your thinking when you write the things you plan to do.

Example:

Lord, when we think life isn't fair, remind us that we are not always fair to others. Sometimes we show more attention to one child or grandchild than another. We know we've been guilty of responding more to the family member who does things our way or to the one who agrees most with us. We pay attention to people who pay attention to us. Help us appreciate the way You lead even when we don't understand or see the end result.

1. Sometimes we need to confess our sins or weaknesses on paper. Write the selfish or mean things you do that have stunted your spiritual growth or harmed your relationship with your spouse.

His Response   *Her Response*

_____   _____

_____   _____

_____   _____

_____   _____

_____   _____

_____   _____

2. Describe a person who has made a positive influence on you or your marriage. How did he or she do it? Was he or she ever selfish or mean? What were his or her good qualities?

His Response   *Her Response*

_____   _____

_____   _____

_____   _____

_____   _____

_____   _____

_____   _____

_____   _____

3. Describe some changes in your heart that would strengthen your marriage.

His Response   *Her Response*

_____   _____

_____   _____

_____   _____

_____   _____

_____   _____

_____   _____

_____   _____

_____   _____

4. Describe some changes in your spouse that you'd like to see happen for his or her good. What can you do to influence a change in his or her life? Remember, nagging will not open someone up to change but will instead close him or her off to anything you say.

His Response   *Her Response*

_____   _____

_____   _____

_____   _____

_____   _____

_____   _____

_____   _____

Marriage-Strengthening Exercises

Sit down and talk.

Find yourself a seat somewhere around the house where you can enjoy one another and do some problem solving (i.e., a porch swing, patio, family room) or talk about things that are not controversial.

Take a blessings inventory.

Get together to make an inventory of your blessings. Practice complimenting your spouse's accomplishments. Contentment and accomplishments enlarge each other.

Take a walk together.

Leave home and take a walk together. Plan a destination.

Treat yourselves to a treat!

Have coffee together (or a banana split) and enjoy a treat and time together.

Plan a little vacation.

Plan a vacation together. Make it far into the future. Sometimes the greatest happiness we get from vacations is not actually being there, but in anticipation of the satisfaction you will have getting there. Future plans will tighten the bond in marriage and inspire you to work together.

Chapter 3

Adam and Eve
LEARNING TO LIVE AFTER THE HONEYMOON

Introduction by Bill and Vonette Bright
Campus Crusade for Christ, Orlando, Florida

We are impressed with this book for many reasons: First, because of its purpose to help encourage and strengthen married couples in the Lord. The enemy has targeted the Christian family, and if he can drive a wedge between husband and wife, he can destroy the Christian testimony of the home, if not the home itself. We believe these solid Bible lessons from biblical characters will make wonderful lessons for Bible classes.

There's a second reason we endorse this book. It's the practical involvement at the end of each chapter. If couples will study the questions throughout together, and work on "Journaling," then work through the "Practical Take-Aways," it will greatly strengthen their marriage. And the applications are tied to the Bible lessons the stories teach.

There's a third reason we are excited about this project. Elmer and Ruth have been married for more than 55 years. Their marriage is a powerful confirmation of their teaching! But more than just having a solid Christian marriage, they have served the Lord together. Ruth is a graduate of Liberty University and Liberty Baptist Theological Seminary, and Elmer has been to several seminaries; but they've prepared together. Isn't *together* a wonderful word? That's what we pray will happen to your marriage, that you and your spouse will be bonded together, just as God said about Adam and Eve: "That they may be one."

Elmer and Ruth have served the Lord together as pastor and wife, Bible college president and wife, professor and professor. Now they want to help you strengthen your marriage. Our prayer is that God will strengthen many marriages for His service and for His glory because of this excellent book.

Learning to Live After the Honeymoon

Genesis 1-5

If ever there was a marriage made in Heaven, it happened when God brought Adam and Eve together, performed the ceremony, and placed them in a perfect environment. He gave them a task to do, and provided for all their needs. Let's set the scene.

Adam and Eve

- Perfectly made for each other by God Himself.

- Perfectly created in God's image.

- Provided a perfect home.

- In perfect relationship with God.

- God Himself was their marriage counselor and always available.

- Had a perfect diet; they were strong and in vibrant health.

- Their "perfect" relationship was still attacked by satan.

Adam was a perfect husband. After all, he was molded by the Master Craftsman Himself—God!

According to Genesis 2:7, how was Adam created?

_____

_____

_____

_____

More than that, Adam had a God-like personality because God said, *"Let Us make man in Our image, according to Our likeness"* (Gen. 1:26). What more could be said about Adam? He was flawless—he had a perfect physique, he was ruggedly handsome, brilliant, emotionally innocent, and other-centered in his heart. If ever there was a perfect candidate to be a perfect husband, it was Adam. Eve also was the perfect wife.

According to Genesis 2:18, why did God create Eve?

_____

_____

_____

_____

Eve was beautiful, gracious, and no doubt had a creative intellect. She was a perfect helpmeet for Adam, equal in divine standing, purpose, and quality of life.

Read Genesis 2:23 to learn how Adam perceived Eve.

_____

_____

_____

_____

What was the pattern God used to create Adam and Eve? Look in Genesis 1:27 for the answer.

_____

_____

_____

_____

Counseling Approach

Adam and Eve were the perfect couple. They were literally made for each other! They had everything it takes for the perfect marriage.

Neither of them brought leftover baggage to the marriage. There were no secrets, no previous love life, and no preconceived ideas of marriage.

God gave them the perfect home, animals to enjoy, new things to discover, and a perfect relationship with Him. He met them every evening for fellowship and a walk in the garden.

God gave them everything they would ever need. They even had the perfect diet and bodies with no disease. They could eat anything they wanted—except one thing.

That one thing cost them the Garden, but Adam and Eve still fulfilled the divine purpose for their marriage.

What was God's great calling for them? Read Genesis 1:27-28.

_____

_____

_____

_____

Think of their responsibilities. They could serve the Lord God by simply being fruitful and multiplying themselves. But God also wanted them to be happy in marriage.

When Adam named all the animals, he saw them male and female; but he did not have a mate. As Adam named the animals, it made him feel alone. God created woman for the happiness of man, and in the same unconditional way, man gives happiness to the woman because a good marriage reflects love within itself as well as outside of itself. Your marriage can be the happiest thing in life, but if you allow rebellion and sin to take root in your marriage, it can be robbed of happiness and fruitfulness.

What was the result of the union of the first marriage? Write what you think the phrase "one flesh" means.

_____

_____

_____

_____

_____

_____

_____

What Eve Brought to Adam:

- She was part of him.

- She was a complement to him.

- She was his counterpart.

- She ended his loneliness.

- She filled him with happiness.

- They were a perfect "fit."

What was the work God gave them?

_____

_____

_____

_____

After God brought the man and woman together, He had a task for them.

According to Genesis 2:15, what did God want them to do?

_____

_____

_____

_____

_____

Can you imagine a farm where there are no weeds, no parasites, and no disease? While Adam did work, it was not treacherous work, nor was it painful, because there were no obstacles. It was successful work, because when the Lord God planted a garden, what plant would refuse to grow? What garden would refuse to produce its fruit?

How Did Eve Assist Adam?

Eve was called to be a helpmeet, which doesn't mean a servant or slave. The word *help* means that what you do, your helper also does. Therefore, as Adam worked in the garden, Eve worked alongside him, helping him in his labor.

What Was the Nature of Adam's Leadership?

The very nature of the word *helpmeet* means that Eve was to help Adam in his work. But that word *helpmeet* implies that Adam was the leader and she was his helper. God had given Adam a task, and He gave Eve to him as his helpmeet.

How Was Eve a Helpmeet?

- She assisted.

- She encouraged.

- She advised.

- She inspired.

- She responded to Adam's leadership.

How Did Adam Display Leadership?

- He accepted Eve's help.

- He listened to her advice.

- He treated her fairly.

- He was grateful for her.

How was their marriage described?

_____

_____

_____

_____

When you look at the marriage of Adam and Eve, how did they get along? First, they were pure and innocent, because the Bible says, *"And they were both naked, the man and his wife, and were not ashamed"* (Gen. 2:25). This implies they were pure in their thoughts, their actions, and in all they did. But also, there was no strife or anger because sin had not yet been introduced into the world. Adam and Eve got along harmoniously with each other because they had peace with God. They lived in *paradise* because Eden was *"the Paradise of God"* (Rev. 2:7). Inasmuch as the word *paradise* means orchard or park, it is a place where everything is beautiful and orderly. Everything was as it should have been.

How did the first couple express their oneness? See Ephesians 5:31.

_____

_____

_____

_____

When the Honeymoon Is Over

How long was it before Adam and Eve sinned?

_____

_____

_____

_____

We don't know how long it was before Adam and Eve sinned. But it probably wasn't very long. As a matter of fact, it may have been less than a month. They had a wonderful honeymoon (the word *honeymoon* means "first moon" or "first month"). Can you imagine going on a honeymoon that was planned by God, paid for by God, and everything was perfect?

How shall a man and wife express their "oneness" today? See Ephesians 5:33.

_____

_____

_____

_____

What Is a Honeymoon?

- The fulfillment of a lifelong dream.

- The sweetest time of marriage.

- Beginning marriage with the best.

- Beginning marriage with the full expression of love.

- The foundation for a future life.

- A prediction of the future.

How Did Satan Get Eve to Make a Bad Choice?

God had told Adam that they could eat of every tree in the garden. But the food they were provided did not include fruit from the tree that was prohibited to them. Food grew on all the trees, and the couple had access to all of the fruit except the one tree in the middle of the garden. It was a special tree.

God had told Adam that he was not to eat of the central tree in the garden. If God told Eve directly not to eat of that tree, that conversation is not recorded in the Bible. It was Adam's responsibility to tell Eve, and he did. Eve knew that she was not supposed to eat of the tree, and she knew that she would die if she did. (By the way, sin was not in the fruit of that one tree. It was in disobeying God.)

It's easy to see how satan found a stronghold. First, satan placed *doubt* in Eve's mind: *"Has God indeed said?"* (Gen. 3:1). Second, satan *denied* what God had said with his reply, *"You will not surely die"* (v. 4). And finally, satan *distorted* what God had said, *"For God knows that in the day you eat of it your eyes will be opened, and you will be like God, knowing good and evil"* (v. 5).

Be careful when making decisions. Your decisions can have a lasting effect on your life and on others for generations. As for Eve, she second-guessed God's purposes and commands concerning the forbidden tree, and satan used this to tempt and deceive her.

Adam chose not to intervene, though he was present the whole time (see Gen. 3:6). Instead, he disobeyed God with open eyes, following Eve into his own curse instead of leading her to obedience.

Why Did Eve Flirt With Temptation?

Eve had everything a woman could want in life. She had a wonderful husband, a perfect environment, and all she wanted to eat. But the fruit on the tree was a temptation to her. What caused her to even go near the tree? Why did she spend time around the one thing God warned about? The woman felt that the tree had something for her that she didn't have. The more she looked at the fruit, the more it became an obsession. And when she could resist it no longer, she took it and ate it and then gave it to her husband.

Genesis 3:6 says, *"When the woman saw that the tree was good for food, that it was pleasant to the eyes, and a tree desirable to make one wise, she took of its fruit and ate. She also gave to her husband with her, and he ate."*

One of the most powerful words in life is *together,* because God put a man and woman together. As companions, a husband and wife can do much for God together. They are uniquely gifted to encourage each other toward good works and a growing faith.

How Did Adam and Eve Respond to Their Sin?

First, since Adam was the head, he knew he was responsible.

According to Genesis 3:12, what did he say?

_____

_____

_____

_____

Adam wanted to blame God for his sin, so he blamed God for giving Eve to him in the first place. But since leadership also influences followers, Eve did the same.

According to Genesis 3:13, who did Eve blame?

_____

_____

_____

_____

Many times marriages are destroyed because the husband or wife will not take responsibility for his or her problems. A husband may rebel when his wife wants him to do what is right. He might blame her for his rebellion. A wife may follow the same practice. What's the problem? They both blame each other, rather than taking responsibility.

What Was the Consequence of Adam's Sin?

Because Adam was given leadership over all things, his one sin conveyed consequences to all of creation.

What Influence Can a Woman Have on a Man?

As in the garden, the woman whom a man loves is a powerful presence in his life. In Adam's case, this power seems to have distracted him from obeying God. But don't forget that in the same way, the spiritual commitment of a wife can also lift her husband.

Did God Leave Them Without Hope?

No! Even though Adam and Eve sinned, God came to them with redemption. First, God clothed them with the skins of an animal. Throughout Christian tradition, teachers have taught that the animal was a lamb because God later required the blood of a lamb to be shed for the covering of sin (John 1:29).

Second, God promised that the seed of Eve would deliver them (Gen. 3:15). When Cain was born, Eve laughed with delight: *"I have acquired a man from the Lord"* (Gen. 4:1). She must have thought that Cain was her deliverer, as well as the deliverer of the human race. But time proved her wrong; Cain killed his brother, Abel. Eventually, Eve conceived again and with hope she said, *"For God has appointed another seed for me"* (Gen. 4:25). But then, even this child, Seth, was not to be the deliverer of the human race. It would be centuries before the Messiah, Jesus Christ, would come. After Seth was born, somehow people realized that it would take time before the Messiah was born, so *"then men began to call on the name of the Lord"* (Gen. 4:26).

Practical Take-Aways

The Sum Total principle.

A marriage represents the sum total of what both husband and wife bring to the union. If either member of the marriage has major character flaws, those weaknesses will ultimately weaken a marriage. Both parties must honestly and realistically assess their strengths and weaknesses together and then make plans to strengthen the marriage, focusing mainly on their strengths. Remember though, for all of its God-given wonders, love tends to be blind. Two lovers seldom acknowledge seriously the character wrinkles in each other before the wedding. Even if they did, it doesn't mean the flaws will or should stop a marriage ceremony. Honesty, communication, and—above all—pure-hearted, loving appreciation for each other should help couples strengthen their union and help prevent problems.

What Happens When You Sin?

- Guilt: *"They knew they were naked"* (Gen. 3:7).

- Pain: *"Multiply your sorrow"* (Gen. 3:16).

- Anxiety about failure: *"You shall not eat of it"* (Gen. 3:17).

- Problems: *"Thistles it shall bring forth"* (Gen. 3:18).

- Loss of fulfillment in work: *"In the sweat of your face"* (Gen. 3:19).

- Lasting results: Something inside you dies.

A helpmeet versus a leader.

The very word *helpmeet* implies a wife is helping her husband. He can't get there without her, and she won't get there alone. Perhaps the descriptive phrase "necessary helpmeet" should be used. They both need each other. They are more together than they are apart.

The final blame game.

Why is it that husbands and wives are quick to blame the other when something goes wrong? Because we are sinners living in a finite world among sinners, and things will often go wrong. So don't be too shaken or surprised by problems. The appliances will wear out, the weeds will grow in every yard, and people will be forgetful and annoying. Don't blame each other when mistakes happen. Just deal with them as graciously as possible and move on. Don't try to find out who is at fault when the physical things around you break down and your mate disappoints you. Be kind. Draw him or her in instead. Share your hurt, but reassure your loved one of your love. Trust one another to build your marriage stronger.

Remember the honeymoon.

One of the best ways to keep a marriage strong is to revisit its foundation and recommit to its promise and hope. Both husband and wife should talk about their dreams, their vows to each other, and their commitment to God.

The "Spare Tire" principle.

You take a spare tire along on trips in case there's a blowout along the road. Take a "spare tire" in case there is a relational blow-up. You don't give up the vacation trip because of a flat tire. You don't give up on a marriage because of an emotional outburst or even serious relational difficulties. Recognize the problem and try to fix it, or let grace put a patch over it and get back on the highway to your destination.

Journaling

Writing your thoughts is a discipline that makes you think clearly about a subject. Since you are serious about developing a strong marriage, use the following questions to guide your thoughts and writings. Remember, writing will clarify your thinking when you write the things you plan to do.

For example:

Lord, thank You for my spouse, my home, and the over-abundance of blessings from You. Help us remember that if You tell us "No," that we need to stay far away so we won't be tempted. We don't want to walk on the edge, but rather, we want to be obedient in the very center of Your will. Don't ever let us be satan's tool in each other's life. Keep our suggestions to each other ordered by You, Lord.

1. What was the most enjoyable thing you remember from your honeymoon? Why was it eventful? How did it influence your marriage?

His Response   *Her Response*

_____   _____

_____   _____

_____   _____

_____   _____

_____   _____

_____   _____

_____   _____

_____   _____

2. What makes your marriage memorable? Why?

His Response   *Her Response*

_____   _____

_____   _____

_____   _____

_____   _____

_____   _____

_____   _____

_____   _____

3. What are the things you expected from marriage that haven't happened? Do you see God's hand in not having them? What things in your marriage are better than you expected? Why?

His Response   *Her Response*

_____   _____

_____   _____

_____   _____

_____   _____

_____   _____

_____   _____

Marriage-Strengthening Exercises

Break out the photo album.

Get out your marriage and wedding pictures. Revisit the events that made you happy.

Renew your vows.

Recommit (repeat) your marriage vows to one another. (This is effective if you have had difficulties in your marriage or have breached it.)

Imagine a second honeymoon.

Plan a "What If" Honeymoon, Part Two. If you had the necessary money, where would you go on a second honeymoon that would bring the two of you closer than ever before and strengthen your marriage?

Chapter 4

Aquila and Priscilla
LEARNING TO WORK TOGETHER

Introduction by John and Margaret Maxwell
Founders of INJOY Group, Atlanta, Georgia

We are delighted to introduce this chapter on Aquila and Priscilla at the request of our dear friends, Elmer and Ruth. We have known the Townses for more than 30 years. Elmer's books on growing churches and Sunday schools were an inspiration to us as we began our life in ministry at a small country church in Hillham, Indiana. Over the years, as we moved from Hillham to Lancaster, Ohio, and then to San Diego, California, Elmer and Ruth became first mentors in ministry and then friends. Like the biblical couple of Aquila and Priscilla, they are loving and giving models of Christ-like living and dedicated Kingdom building.

One of the reasons we enjoy this chapter on Aquila and Priscilla is that they used their excellence in the business community as a platform to reach others for Christ. We connect well with business people, so we feel a kinship with Aquila and Priscilla. Whereas we began our careers in the ministry and God called us out of the local church to reach people in the business community, He called Aquila and Priscilla out of the business community into ministry so they could plant a church in Ephesus.

As you read this chapter, we want to encourage you to follow the example of this godly couple. Whether you are in full-time business, vocational ministry, or another profession, heed God's call wherever it may lead. And mentor godly leaders, as Aquila and Priscilla did Apollos, one of the great post-apostolic church leaders.

May your marriage include ministry with the same kind of impact theirs did.

Learning to Work Together

Acts 18:1-4, 24-28

We don't know where Aquila met his wife, Priscilla, nor do we know how he courted her or anything else about their marriage. We do know they originally came from Pontus, a city on the Black Sea in modern-day Turkey. Since Aquila is a Jewish name, we assume his father chose tentmaking as his occupation when he went through bar mitzvah in a Jewish synagogue. Most people think Priscilla was a Gentile because of her Gentile name. While that is not enough to prove theirs was a mixed marriage, most historians suggest this. For some reason, this ambitious couple left their small Asian town, crossed the Mediterranean into Europe—a different continent and a different culture—to Rome. They settled there, pursuing their occupation of tent making.

But in A.D. 52, Roman Emperor Claudius signed his name to an edict expelling all Jews from Rome, upsetting the life of Aquila and Priscilla forever. Because Jews at that time were contentious (including persecuting their Christian neighbors), the Roman historian Suetonius suggests this was the reason they left Rome. The emperor didn't care if they were causing trouble or not, he just wanted to be rid of them. So all Jews were expelled, including peace-loving Jews like Aquila and Priscilla. They moved their business to Corinth in Greece.

A couple of years later, Paul walked through the shops of the business area of Corinth, where he met Priscilla and Aquila. Because they shared the same occupation, Paul went to work for them, eventually becoming their lifelong friend in ministry.

The Greek word *tentmaker* describes Aquila and Priscilla as owners and operators. As owners, they bought rough goat's hide, employed tentmakers to cut, stitch, and prepare tents, and also employed others as salesmen. A different Greek word for *tentmaker* suggests Paul was a craftsman. He worked for Priscilla and Aquila, who were business owners. Even when Aquila and Priscilla are first seen in the Scriptures, they were working their business together in the markets of Corinth. When they were last seen, they were still working together in ministry. It is clear that Aquila and Priscilla reflected the principles of *marital togetherness* in all ways.

Counseling Approach

Some couples would not be successful or even stay together if they had to work side by side every day. There are usually separate job descriptions. Sometimes one partner takes on the leadership of an area of the business he or she knows best. One may be better at details, where the other is better at dealing with people or understanding the needs of their customers.

Typically, a father and son work together easier than a husband and wife because a son is learning the business from someone who has experience in that business. Sometimes in business, a husband and wife may be equal as partners. Sometimes one must be the leader and the other a follower.

Just as people sometimes disagree with their leader or a fellow worker on the job, so a husband and wife may find themselves in disagreement over job procedures or production. This situation can introduce problems on the job that may be brought into the marriage. If the two of you are going to work together, do your best to leave business issues at work and personal issues at home.

At other times, marital relationships can destroy job relationships. One spouse may be motivated to make it easier for the other, and soon the distribution of the workload is uneven. If one allows the other too much "slack" or has unrealistic standards, the job suffers. It's also easy to assume you can make decisions without consulting your spouse. Remember that you are part of a partnership at work and at home. It's hard when you have to switch between wearing your job hat and your family hat.

Reading about and understanding the God-centered obedience of Aquila and Priscilla can give you hope and direction toward a Christ-like partnership with your spouse at work and at home.

Working together in "tentmaking" can help show you how to work together in ministry. Paul's spiritual insight and practical lessons of daily living can prepare you for times when your marital relationship has to depend on what you've learned from God. Preparation for ministry involves our response to the learning opportunities we receive each day at home and at work. *"He who calls you is faithful, who also will do it"* (1 Thess. 5:24).

What Does It Take for a Husband and Wife to Work Together?

First of all, they must have a mature relationship of respect and understanding. A husband and wife who work together must have as similar an attitude toward one another as two strangers who meet, become friends, and start a business together.

What Does It Take for a Husband and Wife to Work Together?

Couples Who Work Together Successfully...

• Are willing to give more than they receive.

• Are willing to give and take suggestions from each other.

• Respect the talents their partner brings to the job.

• Practice openness about mistakes and problems.

• Enjoy working together.

• Build a marital love that is stronger than financial pressure.

According to Acts 18:2-3, what can we know about a husband and wife being in business together?

_____

_____

_____

_____

What Can Be Said About This Couple's Relationship?

Aquila and Priscilla had determination. They moved to a foreign country after getting married, and worked their business together. When pressure fell on Rome, they stayed together and moved to Corinth. Together, they started their business again. Before their story was finished, they moved to two other cities, starting over at least two more times. Together, they eventually helped start a church.

Aquila and Priscilla employed Paul after they met him in the marketplace. Why would Paul work as a tentmaker when he was called to preach the gospel? Doesn't a church planter need to spend time planting a new church? The answer is very simple: Paul needed money. He didn't want to be a financial burden on the new Corinthian church. He also wanted to demonstrate to the Corinthians that he was self-reliant and would not live off their charity or gifts. But there was a greater reason for Paul's employment by Aquila and Priscilla. Perhaps Paul wanted a testimony of being industrious to the people in Corinth, many of whom were accused of being lazy. Therefore, Paul didn't want a negative image hurting his preaching of the gospel.

What Happened When Paul Came to Live With Aquila and Priscilla?

Paul not only worked for them, he lived in their home and became their friend. Later they traveled with him as fellow workers.

As the three sat eating their meals, Paul taught them the Word of God. As a matter of fact, the couple learned the faith so well that when the popular but inexperienced teacher Apollos arrived in the city, the couple immediately knew he didn't understand the Scriptures.

But there's another side to the faith of this incredible couple.

When Paul suffered persecution, they apparently suffered the same persecution. Paul said, *"Priscilla and Aquila...risked their own necks for my life"* (Rom. 16:3-4). But most importantly, the couple became intimately involved in Paul's ministry to serve Christ. Paul referred to his devoted friends as *"Priscilla and Aquila, my fellow workers in Christ Jesus"* (Rom. 16:3).

> *A marriage is not complete until Jesus is at its center.*

What can we know about a husband and wife serving the Lord together? Look in Acts 18:26.

_____

_____

_____

_____

When Paul lived with Aquila and Priscilla, they went with him each Sabbath to the local synagogue. When Paul separated from the synagogue to start a new church, the couple went with him.

Many couples have deep roots in their local church. Sometimes their family and social relationships are more important than spiritual convictions. When doctrinal problems arise, many couples aren't willing to leave friends and families in a former church to help begin a new church. But that wasn't true of Aquila and Priscilla. When Paul left the synagogue so the church could meet next door, they went with him.

When the Bible says, *"And many of the Corinthians, hearing, believed and were baptized"* (Acts 18:8), we would expect that Aquila and Priscilla were also baptized then. Later, when Paul faced political opposition in Corinth, they also stayed with Paul. *"The Jews with one accord rose up against Paul and brought him to the judgment seat"* (Acts 18:12).

Aquila and Priscilla eventually rose together in the church at Corinth. When Paul left to go to Jerusalem, the couple became prominent in leadership. Almost immediately, Apollos arrived in Corinth from Egypt. As Priscilla and Aquila listened in the synagogue to this mighty man expounding the Scriptures, they felt something was missing.

Apollos did not yet know that Jesus was the Messiah, nor did he know that the Holy Spirit had been given. What did he know? He knew the truth that was taught in the Old Testament, and because he believed what he knew, he had Old Testament salvation. But he didn't have the Holy Spirit. Apparently, only Aquila and Priscilla perceived his ignorance.

How to Strengthen Your Marriage

- Read and study the Word together.

- Talk about the Scriptures as you travel or stay at home.

- Look for ways to apply the Scriptures practically.

- Share thoughts with each other.

- Listen to each other's questions and concerns about Christianity.

- Answer each other's questions with respect and love.

According to Acts 18:26, what did Aquila and Priscilla do for Apollos?

_____

_____

_____

_____

Together this couple invested their lives in a brilliant preacher, and the fruit of their ministry followed Apollos everywhere he preached the Word of God.

It should not be her ministry or his ministry; it should be their ministry

The church was not originally in the house of Aquila and Priscilla. When Paul led the people out of the synagogue, he went to a house that belonged to Titius Justus. However, for reasons unexplained, the church moved out of the house of Titius Justus and into the house of Aquila and Priscilla. Perhaps their business prospered so that they built a larger house that could accommodate the new growing church. Paul noted when writing to the Romans, *"Greet Priscilla and Aquila, my fellow workers in Christ Jesus…Likewise greet the church that is in their house"* (Rom. 16:3-5).

When Emperor Claudius died, Jews were allowed to live in Rome, so Aquila and Priscilla returned to Rome. When they arrived, the first thing they did was to start a church in their new house. They constantly served the Lord together, even in planting a new church.

When a husband and wife are involved in Christian service, what should be their ultimate motivation? Read Romans 16:4.

_____

_____

Aquila and Priscilla finished their marriage well because they finished together. When Paul was a prisoner, 16 years after first meeting the couple in Corinth, he faced death during his second imprisonment in Rome. In Second Timothy, Paul says, *"Greet Priscilla and Aquila, and the household of Onesiphorus"* (2 Tim. 4:19). They were still together and still serving the Lord.

Why Is Priscilla's Name Found First in Some of the Passages?

In our modern churches, it is not unusual for women to be more gifted and aggressive in serving the Lord than their husbands. Some women are more desirous of using their gifts and serving the Lord. Sometimes they must even take the leading role in the spiritual development of their family.

As in all areas of a good and healthy marriage, husbands and wives should be careful not to compete with each other in their ministry efforts. As a matter of fact, all attention in ministry should go to Jesus Christ. A husband and wife don't need to compete but complement each other as "helpmeets" in ministry just as role models Priscilla and Aquila did.

Practical Take-Aways

What can be learned about togetherness in ministry? When a husband and wife serve the Lord together, there are certain guidelines that will help.

Keep Christ as the spotlight in ministry.

Husbands and wives should make sure that Christ is at the center of their marriage. This happens when Jesus becomes first in their lives. It happens when Jesus is more important than anything else.

Be involved as a couple.

If a wife is more gifted, she can encourage her husband to experience the joy of Christian service. He can become involved in ministry—his ministry and her ministry. Each should make it their ministry. God uses people according to their usability.

Complement and support each other's strengths.

When we compete for attention, glory, or even power, we are not working together as "one flesh." Rather, we should complement one another so that the strengths of our mate shine in the service of the Lord.

Be free to minister for God together.

The keywords are *minister* and *together*. Husbands and wives are one, and when they minister together, they fulfill God's plan for marriage. With the same goals in ministry and the same desire to serve the Lord, couples can use their complementing spiritual gifts for greater results.

Journaling

Writing your thoughts is a discipline that makes you think clearly about a subject. Since you are serious about developing a strong marriage, use the following questions to guide your thoughts and writings. Remember, writing will clarify your thinking when you write the things you plan to do.

Example:

Lord, thank You for guiding my spouse and me in Your direction and to each other for Your service. While we work together at home, Father, help us to remember that You are the center of our lives, and that is where our happiness lies. While we work together in our jobs, help us to remember that all glory and honor are Yours, and reveal Your leadership in our choices. We love You and enjoy serving You together.

1. Describe a pleasant mutual task you and your spouse have worked on together.

His Response   *Her Response*

_____   _____

_____   _____

_____   _____

_____   _____

_____   _____

_____   _____

2. Describe an unpleasant working relationship between you and your spouse. Why was it unpleasant? How could the situation have been improved?

His Response   *Her Response*

_____   _____

_____   _____

_____   _____

_____   _____

_____   _____

_____   _____

3. What would be the perfect circumstance where you and your spouse could work together?

His Response   *Her Response*

_____   _____

_____   _____

_____   _____

_____   _____

_____   _____

_____   _____

Marriage-Strengthening Exercises

Make someone you know a prayer project.

Perhaps you know couples who seems to work well together in business during the week, but not at home. Make them a "prayer project." You will perhaps learn some valuable lessons and strengthen your marriage as you pray for them.

Read a book on leadership.

Read a book on leadership that will help you learn more about the tasks of leading and following. Share the results with your spouse. Talk about how you would apply these principles if or when you work together on a project.

Suggested reading:

Developing the Leader Within You by John Maxwell

The 21 Irrefutable Laws of Leadership by John Maxwell

Developing the Leaders Around You by John Maxwell

The 8 Laws of Leadership by Elmer Towns

Volunteer as a couple.

Volunteer to work on a project together at a church or community agency. Apply the principles you've learned in this chapter and from your marriage-strengthening projects.

Chapter 5

Xerxes and Esther
LEARNING TO LIVE WITH MINIMAL CHOICES

Introduction by Ed and Donna Hindson
Institute of Biblical Studies
Liberty University Lynchburg, Virginia

One of the most amazing couples in the Bible is Xerxes and Esther. Esther was a believer who was willing to face death to save God's people. Xerxes was like a lot of men today—stubborn and determined to have his own way. But in the end, Xerxes did what was right. This is a wonderful story of how God blends two different personalities together to accomplish His will.

Elmer and Ruth have beautifully captured the relationship between Xerxes and Esther. The challenges this couple faced are like those many couples face today in blended marriages involving both believers and unbelievers. As you read their amazing story, may God encourage your heart with the fact that He can bring great blessings from a difficult situation.

As we minister to others in teaching, counseling, and writing, we have met many couples like Xerxes and Esther. Their difficulties and challenges may seem overwhelming at first, but God can still accomplish great things in their lives. We pray He will use the story of this couple to lift your hearts and strengthen your marriage.

Learning to Live With Minimal Choices

Esther 4:1-7:10

What do you do when you find yourself in desperate circumstances where you can't do anything about your situation? A husband or wife may feel like an outsider if they live or work with in-laws. Or maybe a wife feels like she is in a prison, raising her husband's children from a former marriage. Perhaps you feel in bondage because of poverty, or limited education, or a debilitating handicap, or a mate with a terminal sickness who desperately needs 24-hour attention.

This was Esther's situation. She was a woman who seemingly had no choices in life. As an orphan, she had little control over her destiny. As a refugee in a foreign land, she was dominated by a foreign culture. She was taken—apparently against her will—into the king's harem and had little choice about the man she married. Sometimes people find themselves living in places they haven't chosen, associating with people they don't desire, and facing problems they can't solve. When Esther couldn't choose the type of life she wanted to live, she decided one thing—Esther chose what type of person she'd become.

Some people marry with a distinct set of expectations, only to find their life very different from what they expected. The story of Xerxes and Esther gives some guidance on how to make things work when you have no control over your circumstances.

Counseling Approach

God loves you and has a wonderful plan for your life. Orphaned, adopted, or married to a king, God has a plan for your life. God governs the preparation and the presentation of our lives for service, not just circumstances (Rom. 8:28).

> You have a job to do. Only God knows the outcome. Obey Him. People tend to make excuses about their background as an excuse for not doing something in life. Don't let your circumstances govern your behavior. Don't make excuses. God chooses the weak things of this world to confound the mighty (see 1 Cor. 1:27-29). Take your strength and courage from God and use it for Him.

How Did Esther Come to Marry Xerxes?

Xerxes (his Greek name) was the king of Persia, the greatest empire in the world. He was also called Ahasuerus (his Hebrew name) by the Jews. Secular history tells us that he ruled Persia from 486 to 465 B.C. His empire stretched from India to Ethiopia, but his real passion was to conquer Greece, the center of Western civilization. Xerxes made hard decisions that made him great, but he also made rash decisions that kept him from ruling the known world. One of these rash decisions was made during a six-month banquet given for his leadership.

How Did Esther Come to Marry Xerxes? Everything was right in the huge palace on the banks of the Eulai River. From the shining black and white floor tiles rose great white marble columns. Flowing canopy veils of white, green, blue, and purple hung from the ceiling. When the guests had eaten all they could eat, drank all the wine they could drink, and nothing was left to excite them, Xerxes made a rash decision and called for his beautiful wife, Vashti, to give his audience another thrill. She said, "No!"

Vashti embarrassed her husband in public, so the king's advisors goaded him to divorce her. Xerxes listened to them and made another rash decision—He divorced her. The following year, Xerxes once again made a rash decision by forcing an attack at Thermopylae, only to be defeated at the Bay of Salamis, where history was changed. The East would not defeat the West. When Xerxes returned home in defeat, he was probably looking for comfort and companionship from his wife, but the queen was indisposed.

Again, Xerxes listened to his counselors. They planned a beauty pageant to choose the next queen. *"Let beautiful young virgins be sought for the king; and let the king appoint officers...that they may gather all the beautiful young virgins...then let the young woman who pleases the king be queen instead of Vashti"* (Esther 2:2-4).

Throughout the kingdom, young girls were captured, kidnapped, or forced to enter the contest to see if they pleased the king. According to Esther 2:8, one of these girls was Esther. The word *taken* in this verse suggests Esther was forced against her will. There was no cry when Esther was taken because she was an orphaned girl, a captive from a foreign land, a girl who was disenfranchised with no civil rights.

Even though it seemed Esther had nothing to live for, what were her prospects?
Look in Galatians 1:3-4 for the answer.

_____

_____

_____

_____

As Esther was waiting for her talent contest with the king, her family didn't forsake her. Mordecai, a cousin who raised her, checked daily to see how she was doing.

According to Esther 2:11, what did Mordecai do out of concern for his cousin?

_____

_____

_____

_____

When you have no control over circumstances in your life, it's good to know someone cares about you and calls from time to time. When Esther went into the palace, cousin Mordecai had counseled her that she should not reveal her people or family (Esther 2:10). No one knows the motive for Mordecai telling her to keep her Jewish ancestry a secret. Racism prevailed in that day, and prejudice might have segregated her—or worse, she might have been executed. It was terrible that Esther had no control over her life, but to make matters worse, she couldn't even tell people who she was.

According to First Corinthians 4:19, what should your attitude be when you feel you have no control over your circumstances?

_____

_____

_____

_____

Read about Paul in Romans 1:10 and 15:32 when he planned to go to Rome. What was his attitude?

_____

_____

_____

_____

Each young lady was offered anything she needed to please the king. Some chose the best of perfumes, others chose oil.

According to Esther 2:15, what did Esther choose?

_____

_____

_____

_____

Your greatest asset in life is not what you have in your hands but what you have in your heart. Esther relied on this inner beauty and spirit to capture the heart of the king.

The greatest attraction is not always the outer woman but rather the inner spirit and grace. A woman's character is what truly endures and stands the test of time.

In Esther 2:17, what was the result of the beauty pageant?

_____

_____

_____

_____

The purpose of this story is not how Esther married Xerxes. There was another plot developing in the Book of Esther. Haman was the prime minister in Xerxes' palace. One day as Haman walked through the city of Shushan, Mordecai refused to bow to Haman. So Haman vowed not only to punish Mordecai but also to exterminate every Jew living in the Persian Empire, which, at that time, would have eliminated every Jew in the world!

Esther's name means "Star," unseen in the daylight, but a guiding beacon in the night.

As Haman passed several papers to the king to sign, one sealed the destruction of the Jews. The king's signature proclaimed anyone who killed a Jew could keep his property, home, or possessions. Since the law of Medes and Persians was an irreversible law, another hasty decision by Xerxes would have disastrous results on the Jews—and ultimately upon Xerxes himself.

What Was the Response of the Jews?

The announced Persian holocaust was devastating news to the Jews, and they began *"fasting, weeping, and wailing"* (Esther 4:3).

Mordecai agonized over this decree. In Esther 4, what does it say he did?

_____

_____

_____

_____

When Esther saw Mordecai in sackcloth at the palace gates, she sent clothes to him. Mordecai sent a message back to Esther to explain the serious situation, asking her to become involved in a solution.

According to Esther 4:13, what was his warning to her?

_____

_____

_____

_____

Mordecai had faith that if she didn't help, God would deliver them by some other means. He also knew that just because Esther had kept her racial background hidden, when the purge came, she would not be exempted.

Yet in Esther 4:14, Mordecai asked Esther a very prophetic question.
What was the question?

_____

_____

_____

_____

Esther may have thought she was disenfranchised, with no power, no connections, and no choices to make. But she had a few things going for her, and she used them for God's glory.

Making It Work When You Have No Choice

- Esther couldn't refuse to marry the king.

- She couldn't return to her homeland.

- She couldn't live with her family.

- She couldn't practice her religion.

- She couldn't go to the king with her problems…but Esther chose to submit to God.

We can always choose to serve the Lord. Look in Ephesians 5:17. How do we begin with our choice to follow God?

_____

_____

We can always choose to serve the Lord. Look in Ephesians 5:17. How do we begin with our choice to follow God?

Mordecai wanted Esther to go to the king to get the decree reversed. Maybe Mordecai didn't understand that the law of the Medes and Persians couldn't be reversed, but he felt in his heart that she could do something to help.

People who barged into the king's presence to demand his time and energy could be severely punished, even executed. Those who appeared in the royal court had to wait until the king held out his scepter to them. Since the king held the power of life and death, when he held out his scepter to the person, he granted them the right of an interview. If he refused, the person was taken away and killed. Esther knew all of this, but for a woman who had no other choice, she chose to serve God and her people. *"If I perish, I perish!"* she said (Esther 4:16).

What Was Esther's First Step?

What is the first thing you do when faced with a severe problem? You turn to God. Esther told Mordecai, *"Go...fast for me...For three days, night or day"* (Esther 4:16).

The message of Esther is this: When you can't practice your faith and can't even speak the name of God, He is there for you like a star. You can't see Him in the daylight, but He is there for you in the dark night of tribulation.

If we choose to follow the Lord, what is the first thing we must give Him according to Romans 12:1-2?

_____

_____

_____

The character of a woman can be seen in the quality of the decisions she makes when circumstances are dire and consequences are threatening. Esther took the initiative. Only she could do for the Jews what no one else could do.

How Did Esther React to This Problem?

Esther used common sense. Notice the practical ways she approached the problem.

She dressed for success. Esther dressed for her presentation to the king. *"Esther put on her royal robes"* (Esther 5:1).

She stood at the right place. She *"stood in the inner court"* (5:1). Notice that Esther didn't send the message to her husband by a servant, she didn't invite him to dinner by a written invitation, nor did she pray that God would place a desire in Xerxes' heart to come see her. She took the initiative by standing at the right place at the marble column, which was the place where those seeking to see the King stood.

She took the right approach. As Esther was waiting on the king, he saw her beautiful clothes and remembered his love for her. Beckoning her, Esther approached the king with respect and dignity. *"Esther went near and touched the top of the scepter"* (5:2).

She provided the right setting. Esther invited the king to come to her palace for a banquet. In the quietness and privacy of her home, she would ask the king to spare the Jews. Not only did Esther want the king to come to a banquet, she also included Haman in her invitation. She planned to have all the people together so everyone could face the issue together.

When Facing Tough Decisions...

• Know you are a part of God's plan on earth.

• Do not try to find the easy way out.

• Claim God's grace and guidance.

•• Commit the results to God.

She created an element of suspense. When the king and Haman came to the banquet the first night, Esther didn't tell the king what she wanted. She got him to promise to return the next night for another banquet. She wanted his full attention.

Esther, Mordecai, and all the Jews were praying. How did God answer their prayers? God works in the hearts of people to arrange circumstances. The next time you pray concerning a problem, remember there are many ways God can answer your prayers.

How Were Esther's Prayers Answered?

Haman was impulsive. Haman arrived at work one morning and Mordecai was there. Again, he wouldn't bow to him. Infuriated, Haman decided to do something immediately instead of waiting for all the Jews to be eliminated. Haman had a large gallows built to hang Mordecai.

The king discovered Mordecai. After the king and Haman left Esther's first night banquet, the king couldn't sleep. When the king couldn't sleep, he called for his musty, old records to be read to him. Years before, there was an assassination attempt on the king's life. This was the first time he had heard of it, though. Reading further, the king found out that Mordecai had saved his life, so he determined to do something about it the next day.

The following morning when Haman came into the king's presence, Xerxes asked him, "How can I honor someone who needs special commendation?" Haman thought that Xerxes was talking about him, so he suggested the king should honor the person by putting royal robes on him, letting him ride the king's animals throughout the city, and having a dignitary proclaim to everyone, "This is the one who the king would honor."

"You do that to Mordecai," Xerxes told Haman. Doesn't God have an interesting sense of humor?

When Haman got home from spending the day honoring Mordecai, the king's servants appeared to escort him to Esther's second banquet. When they arrived at Esther's palace, the king didn't want to eat; he wanted to get straight to Esther's request. Then Esther told her husband Xerxes about the threat to the Jews.

According to Esther 7:3-4, what did she ask of the king?

_____

_____

_____

_____

_____

King Xerxes flew into a rage. He asks a poignant question of Esther, "Who is responsible for attempting to destroy the Jews?"

"Your adversary and enemy is this wicked Haman," Esther said, pointing a finger at Haman.

Then one of the chamberlains stepped forward and suggested, "Look at the gallows that is 75 feet tall." Xerxes said, "Hang him!" And it was done. On this occasion, God used the king's rash decision to do His will, and Haman was killed on the very gallows he constructed to kill Mordecai.

Why Was There Still a Problem?

Even though Haman was eliminated, the problem did not go away. There was still the irreversible law of the Medes and Persians.

What should your attitude be when you can't accomplish your goals? Read James 4:13-15.

_____

_____

_____

_____

So Esther in her wisdom devised a higher law. A new law was written that allowed the Jews to protect themselves when the day of infamy arrived. The Jews could kill anyone who attacked them and keep the attacker's money and houses. The law gave the Jews equal standing with their enemy. The king signed the law and made the field level for all.

The Results

The Jews got together to defend themselves.

75,000 enemies were destroyed.

Practical Take-Aways

Here's what to do when you feel trapped by your circumstances.

Maybe life looks dark and things are frustrating because you have no good choices. Does it look like every path leads into deeper trouble? Fortunately, when you're in a deep, dark hole, the only place you can look is up. *So look up to God when you have troubles.*

Amazing things happen when you look to God.

You get a new perspective on your problem. *You can see your problems through God's eyes.* He knows the future and He can show it to you. You'll have *God's eternal view*—a long-range view. That means you can evaluate your problems from His values or with His expectations. Doing this will help you to better size up your situation.

When you look to God, you'll begin to see God's purpose for your life.

God has a plan for your life. Maybe you'll hear the same admonitions Esther heard from Mordecai when he said, "You are born into God's kingdom for such a time and problem as this." Evaluate your problem in light of God's ultimate plan for your life.

Remember that God is a problem solver.

He specializes in impossibilities. In this step, you'll learn the Christian life is always practical and workable. God never dabbles in a theoretical religion. When His creatures sinned in disobedience, God didn't think up some abstract solution. No! Jesus became flesh, took on our limitations, died for our sins, and will deliver us—if we let Him. He'll deliver you, too, if you'll let Him.

Journaling

Writing your thoughts is a discipline that makes you think clearly about a subject. Since you are serious about developing a strong marriage, use the following questions to guide your thoughts and writings. Remember, writing will clarify your thinking when you write the things you plan to do.

For example:

Help us remember all timing is Your timing, O Father. Sometimes we wonder and just can't find rhyme or reason for the situations of the moment, but You give peace when we yield to You. When sorrow or trials or fear or danger stop us in our tracks, help us, Father, to understand that Your ways are not our ways, and our timing is not perfect. Help us prepare and take time to come into Your presence. We want to be beautiful inside, like Esther, and useable in Your timing to make a difference.

1. Write some experiences where God perfectly worked out the details of a situation that could have been bad. Perhaps this was an instance when you thought everything would fail. How did He do it? Take this opportunity to praise Him on paper for all His goodness and mercy.

His Response

Her Response

_____   _____

_____   _____

_____   _____

_____   _____

_____   _____

_____   _____

2. Write a few lessons you think you should learn to be beautiful on the inside.

His Response   *Her Response*

_____   _____

_____   _____

_____   _____

_____   _____

_____   _____

_____   _____

3. Make a list of the things in your life you can't control that frustrate you and keep you from doing more for God and others. What can you do about them? What will be your response to them?

His Response   *Her Response*

_____   _____

_____   _____

_____   _____

_____   _____

_____   _____

_____   _____

4. What principles have you learned about yielding to the will of God? How did you learn God's will? What is God's will for your life?

His Response

_____

_____

_____

_____

_____

_____

Her Response

_____

_____

_____

_____

_____

_____

Marriage-Strengthening Exercises

Seek counsel.

When you are frustrated with your circumstances, get counsel from someone who knows you best.

Study the Bible—alone or in a group.

Do a Bible study on the will of God. Look up verses that discuss God's will. As you learn the principles of finding and knowing God's will for all believers, you'll find God's unique will for your own life.

Communicate with your spouse about your frustrations.

Make plans (a date or special dinner) to talk to your mate about one of your frustrations over a present circumstance. Remember, Esther knew she had to talk to her husband about the problem. Both of you should do the same.

Chapter 6

Samson and Delilah
LEARNING FROM BAD CHOICES

Introduction by Tim and Julie Clinton
American Association of Christian Counselors
Lynchburg, Virginia

We both attended Liberty University and were students of Elmer Towns, so we know his Bible teaching and commitment to ministry. Now we live next door to Elmer and Ruth, and we know their commitment to the Lord. So it's a privilege to write this introduction for Samson and Delilah.

While we were at Liberty University, there were many young men and women who fell in love, got married, and made a commitment to serve Christ as we did.

Sadly, too many of them fell by the wayside and are not serving the Lord or living for Him today.

Marriage is tough enough when you have two reasonably healthy individuals working together to keep their love alive. And if you've tasted of love in marriage, you know that all couples will go through periods of disaffection—times when you don't feel close. Even more, in today's time-starved world, so much competes for or tears at our hearts. The good news is that no matter what your marital story is, your relationship isn't beyond the love, care, and reach of God. He can make a way. May God give you *the marriage you've always wanted.*

Learning from Bad Choices

Judges 14-16

If there was ever a good man with a woman problem, it was Samson. Almost everything we know about Samson relates to the questionable women in his life. In the Scriptures, his problem (or his life story) is centered on three women. First, he married a Philistine woman but didn't live with her. Next, his life was defined by a prostitute from Gaza in the Philistine country. Finally, his ministry was leveled by Delilah, who was bribed by five Philistine rulers to deliver Samson to them. Because of his weakness for women, he couldn't resist Delilah.

How can Samson's life be described? Both the limitations of his ministry and his ultimate defeat were the result of the bad choices he made.

Counseling Approach

Usually, it's easier to see potential problems in someone else's relationship rather than in our own.

Have you ever had a friend who pulls you down or wears you out? What does that say about you? Do you let them do it, or can you stand your ground and be true to yourself? Some people are strong in many ways, and at the same time, let others control their lives.

Samson was a very strong man, and he made a serious vow. The problem is, we usually fall in areas where we *think* we'll never fall. *"Let him who thinks he stands take heed lest he fall"* (1 Cor. 10:12).

Why Do People Make Bad Choices?

As a young man, Samson began life with great hope, but it ended badly. He seemed to have a passion for God but expressed his passion in the wrong ways. At times, Samson defended God's honor, while at other times, he compromised his faith. The worst thing about his compromise was that Samson flirted with the enemies of God and submitted himself to them.

Why Do People Make Bad Choices?

1. Habit: A lifestyle of bad choices.

2. Weakness: They aren't strong enough to say no.

3. Ignorance: They don't understand the alternatives.

4. Uneducated or Naivety: They were never taught to make good choices.

5. Example: They follow people they mistake as heroes.

6. Pleasure: They are ruled by the lust of the flesh, lust of the eyes, and the pride of life.

7. Comfort: Good choices are hard to make, but bad choices are easy.

A bank president had begun a small-town bank, and when the big city moved out to his area, he built the bank into an area-wide financial giant. As he was retiring, a young vice-president who aspired to his job interviewed him. "How did you build this bank to such great proportions?" the young man asked. "Good decisions," the old banker replied. Not being satisfied, the young VP asked, "How did you learn to make good decisions?" "Bad decisions," the old banker answered.

What Is a Nazarite?

Samson was a Nazarite. The word *Nazarite* comes from *Nazar*, "to vow." A Nazarene is a person who has made a vow to God. A person could be a Nazarite for a short period of time or for a lifetime. Apparently, Samson and John the Baptist were lifelong Nazarenes. When people made a vow to God, they usually made an outward pledge to demonstrate their sincerity. Originally, God gave three stipulations to accompany the Nazarite vow.

According to Numbers 6:2-6, what were these stipulations?

_____

_____

_____

_____

Outward Symbols of a Nazarite

• He shall not cut his hair.

• He shall not eat grapes or have an intoxicating drink.

• He shall not touch a dead body.

What Was the Result of Taking the Nazarite Vow?

While people make all types of vows, some keep them—but some do not. The Nazarite vow of Samson was especially blessed of God. *"The child grew, and the Lord blessed him. And the Spirit of the Lord began to move upon him"* (Judg. 13:24-25).

If you were to see a man like Samson beginning his ministry today, you would probably think he was a young man with a great opportunity. He not only separated himself from the world, but this man seemed to be touched by God for ministry. He came from the right home, had good parents, and had a promising future in Christian service.

What Was the Basis of Samson's Poor Choices?

What Was the Result of Taking the Nazarite Vow?

A godly man should choose to marry a godly woman. But this wasn't Samson's course. Samson *"saw a woman in Timnah...and told his father and mother, saying, 'I have seen a woman...get her for me as a wife'"* (Judg. 14:1-2). Rather than spending his time with the godly women of Israel, Samson was attracted to a daughter of the Philistines (Israel's enemy). This is no Romeo and Juliet story where boy and girl are both good kids whose parents are fighting. The Philistines were an ungodly nation given over to idol worship (which implies demonic influences) and sexual immorality. Samson was smitten by sexual appetite for a Philistine woman. He made a choice by an outward appearance.

Why do we usually fall into temptation? Read James 1:14-15.

_____

_____

_____

_____

_____

_____

_____

What Was Wrong with Samson's Choice?

- Wrong desire. *"She pleases me"* (Judges 14:3).

- Wrong plan. *"Get her for me"* (v. 3).

- Wrong option. Samson's father said, *"Is there no woman among the daughters of your brethren, or among all my people?"* (v. 3).

- Wrong passion. *"She pleases me well"* (v. 3).

What has God promised to us when we are tempted?
Go to First Corinthians 10:13 for the answer.

_____

_____

_____

_____

Why Is the Story of the Lion Included?

When Samson went to visit his future wife, he walked through a vineyard where a lion attacked him.

In Judges 14:6, what does it say Samson did?

_____

_____

_____

_____

While this seems like an innocent story, it is included for more reasons than to demonstrate Samson's strength. Most of all, it demonstrates how he lived on the edge. Eating grapes was against his Nazarite vow, so why was he in that vineyard? Samson is similar to Eve circling the tree of forbidden fruit. While the text doesn't say that he ate grapes, it certainly is suggested.

The next time Samson visited his future wife, he walked through the same vineyard. *"He turned aside to see the carcass of the lion"* (Judg. 14:8). Bees had formed a hive inside the carcass and he took the honey from it, breaking the second part of his vow by touching a dead body. Even as he came close to losing the source of his power, did Samson realize what he was doing? After he broke two of the three Nazarite vows, he still had his power. He was probably thinking, "God didn't mean what He threatened."

The wedding of Samson apparently lasted one week because the Hebrew word for marriage suggests that it was a series of wedding feasts. Also, it is the word for a "drinking" feast. During this feast, Samson entertained the men at the feast by giving them a riddle.

According to Judges 14:14, what was the riddle?

_____

_____

_____

_____

They couldn't solve this riddle even though, day after day, they suggested different answers, so they got Samson's wife to help them out. She did help them, proving that she was more loyal to her Philistine friends than to her new husband. She besieged Samson to tell her the solution to the riddle. At first, Samson was able to resist her charm. But after she threw herself on him, she was finally able to get the answer.

According to Judges 13:16, what did she say to Samson to convince him to tell her the answer?

_____

_____

_____

_____

A couple should learn from this negative example. Never threaten your spouse with "I won't love you if…" Never say, "I'll leave you if you don't…" Any relationship built on threats is weak, and the one who threatens is extremely immature.

What should our attitude be when we see our mate face a temptation or fall to one? Read Galatians 6:1-2.

_____

_____

_____

_____

Ultimately, Samson told his wife the answer, she told the Philistines, and they demanded the prize money for solving the riddle. As a result, Samson's anger led to violence. He lashed out at them and, to get money to pay off his wages, he killed 30 men (see Judg. 14:19).

Samson and Delilah

To any man who has made a vow to the Lord, satan will send along a Delilah to test him.

But Samson knew better. Let's not blame Delilah for it all. Samson was strong of body, but weak in lifestyle. He was in the wrong location, and he was with the wrong crowd. Samson had already broken his Nazarite vow twice, but "three strikes and you're out" eventually came true for him.

What Does Anger Do to Those We Love?

Samson's wife begged him for the answer until he gave in. Then he reacted angrily to her and to the Philistines at the wedding. He killed 30 men to pay off the riddle's prize and stomped away, leaving his new bride at home.

According to Judges 15:6, what happened to her?

_____

_____

_____

_____

_____

_____

_____

How Do People Respond to Bad Choices?

- They become violently angry. See Judges 14:19 for an example.

- They strike out at an enemy. See Judges 15:4-5 for examples.

- They alienate the one they love. See Judges 14:20 for an example.

- They isolate themselves. See Judges 15:1-6 for an example.

Samson and the Harlot at Gaza

It took awhile for Samson to get over the loss of his wife and his angry outburst at the Philistines. We don't know what he did in the interim, but the next story in Scripture describes Samson on his way to the Philistine city of Gaza to visit a harlot (Judg. 16:1-3).

Why Was This a Bad Choice?

He broke the seventh commandment, he had the audacity to go to the enemy, and he put himself in mortal danger. But God protects fools, and Samson should have been thankful for that.

In the middle of the night, it seemed God awakened Samson, and he realized that the enemy had surrounded the house of the prostitute. The city gates were locked, and he had no way to escape. The Philistines were poised to attack and kill him. Miraculously, Samson broke down the city gates, put them on his back, and carried them away. Again, Samson narrowly escaped. Because he was not immediately judged for each bad choice, he didn't repent and change his ways. Although he got himself out of trouble, he never learned from his mistakes, so he fell back into the same problem. With each mishap, Samson got closer and closer to his ultimate downfall and disaster.

According to James 4:7, what should be the first thing you do when tempted?

_____

_____

_____

_____

_____

What should we remember, according to First John 1:8, 10, when we think
we are above temptation?

_____

_____

_____

_____

_____

What should we do when we fall to a temptation? Look in First John 1:9
for the answer.

_____

_____

_____

_____

_____

_____

How to Break the Cycle of Bad Decisions

- Study how to make good decisions.

- Study the consequences of bad decisions.

- Analyze your actions by Scripture.

- Call a moratorium—a moment for waiting—before making any decisions.

- Write the pros and cons of each decision to become more objective.

- Examine your motives that lead to bad decisions.

- Make a list of the ten worst decisions you've ever made and list all the causes. Learn from them.

- Make a list of the ten best decisions you've ever made and look for a pattern you can follow in the future.

What was it about Philistine women that attracted Samson? Was it their facial features? Was it the color of their skin or hair? Or was it their accent? Just as Samson had previously made bad decisions in seeking a Philistine wife and visiting a prostitute in Gaza, his next stumbling block was Delilah: *"He loved a woman… whose name was Delilah"* (Judg. 16:4). If you don't solve a moral problem in your life, it will eventually return again and again until you master it or it masters you.

What Did Samson's Enemies Know About Him?

Every person has a weakness. Somewhere there is a weak link in the chain. Samson's weak link was women. It's too bad when your enemies know your weakness better than you; it means they're stronger than you and can capture you.

According to Judges 16:5, what did the Philistines ask Delilah to do?

_____

_____

_____

_____

_____

_____

Why Was Delilah Not Right for Samson?

If Delilah loved Samson, she would have fought for him and protected him. But her love wasn't deep, if she had any love at all, for she deceived and destroyed him.

Why Was Delilah Able to Trick Samson?

- He was excited.

- He was lustful.

- He was spiritually ignorant.

What were Samson's close calls?

On three occasions, Delilah asked Samson to tell her his weakness. On three occasions, Samson lied to her. Each time he lied, he got closer to telling her the secret of his strength: his hair. Just as each woman brought Samson progressively closer to destruction, so did each of Samson's lies to Delilah.

The Three Lies of Samson

1. "Tie me with seven green vines."

2. "Tie me with new rope."

3. "Weave may seven locks into a loom."

Samson should have been smart enough to know Delilah was setting him up. After he told her that seven green vines would render him helpless, she tied him with green vines and then called in the Philistines to capture him. After he defeated them, he should have fled for his life. But like a moth flying dangerously close to the flame, he couldn't help but go back for more.

What Was Delilah's Response When She Got Caught?

She was deceptively brilliant. The first time she got caught, Samson didn't run away—but neither did she. Instead, she blamed Samson.

What did she say? Read Judges 16:10 for the answer.

_____

_____

_____

_____

_____

_____

Delilah did more than complain about Samson deceiving her. She belittled him and turned her vicious tongue on him.

According to Judges 16:16, what did she do?

Eventually, Delilah got the answer she wanted. He told her that when his hair was cut, he would be powerless. When Delilah realized he was being honest, she called the lords of the Philistines and the trap was set to capture this powerful man who was blind to danger because of his all-consuming lust.

Perhaps Samson really believed his strength was in his hair, but his real strength was in the vow he made to the Lord. Is that like us today? Many of us believe our strength is in our tithing, church attendance, or some other outward conformity to God. We boast, *"I can do all things"* but forget to complete the verse, *"... through Christ who strengthens me"* (Phil. 4:13).

Delilah put Samson to sleep in her lap and then called a barber to cut his hair. After walking dangerously close to the edge, Samson finally fell.

What Was Samson's Last Opportunity to Finally Make a Good Choice?

During a drinking banquet, the Philistines wanted to be entertained by Samson. But it was not just that—they wanted to humiliate him. So a young boy led the blind giant of God, now reduced to a stumbling wimp, before the multitude. Samson was so humiliated he wanted to die; but he wanted to take his enemies with him.

He asked the young boy to place him where he could touch the pillars of the great hall. With both hands on the pillars, Samson knew that if he destroyed one pillar, the whole temple would collapse.

With both his hands on the pillars, Samson prayed, *"Strengthen me just one more time"* (Judg. 16:28, author's translation). It's rewarding to know that in the end, Samson finally made a good choice. However, it's discouraging to know that it was his last prayer.

What Samson Didn't Know

- He couldn't bounce back. *"I will shake myself free"* (Judg. 16:20).

- His spiritual strength was gone. *"He did not know that the Lord had departed from him"* (v. 20).

- He didn't know they would blind him. *"The Philistines took him and put out his eyes"* (v. 21).

- He didn't know they would put him in prison. *"They bound him with bronze fetters"* (v. 21).

- He didn't know they would humiliate him. *"Call for Samson, that he may perform for us"* (v. 25).

In a courageous act, Samson destroyed the temple, which was the glory of the Philistines. *"So the dead that he killed at his death were more than he had killed in his life"* (Judg. 16:30).

What should be our attitude after we are restored, and what is God's response to our attitude? Read First John 1:7.

_____

_____

_____

Practical Take-Aways

Life is filled with choices.

No matter who you are, the most important thing about your success with God is measured by the choices you've made to follow God. And your weaknesses in life are the result of bad choices. To have a better life doesn't involve more money, a better home, or a better job. It doesn't even include a better marriage. If you could begin today to make better choices—outstanding decisions—you'd have a better life.

There's usually weakness in strength.

Sometimes the strongest thing can't be used because it isn't flexible. Samson was the strongest man physically, but inwardly he was weak. Samson couldn't say "no" to his weakness. He needed to learn the following truth: *"I can win any victory— including the victory over sexual addictions—through the Lord who strengthens me"* (Phil. 4:13, author's paraphrase).

The enemy knows your weakness.

When the Philistines couldn't defeat Samson in battle, they defeated him spiritually. Does the enemy know your weakness? Does he use it against you? After Paul confessed his weakness in Romans 7, he then relied on God for victory: *"I thank God—through Jesus Christ our Lord!"* (Rom. 7:25).

God is the God of second chances.

After Samson was defeated, and after he was in prison, God gave him a second chance. Why? Because Samson confessed his sin and prayed for God's help. Then God used him a "second time." But notice the difference: God used him in a different way and with different results. God's use of Samson had a different testimony among the believers.

Journaling

Writing your thoughts is a discipline that makes you think clearly about a subject. Since you are serious about developing a strong marriage, use the following questions to guide your thoughts and writings. Remember, writing will clarify your thinking when you write the things you plan to do.

Example:

Lord, help us to encourage and enrich the lives of those around us. We don't want to be a negative influence or even help the enemy to destroy a person. We want to be a nourishing influence. Help us to be careful with the promises and vows we make. Help us never to forget them. Thank You for keeping Your promises, and guide us in Your ways.

1. Think of a strong person you know who fell to a weakness. What could have "saved" him or her? What could you have done that you didn't do? What would you do next time if the same circumstances arose?

His Response   *Her Response*

_____   _____

_____   _____

_____   _____

_____   _____

_____   _____

_____   _____

2. Describe your strengths (not to brag, but to be objective). How can you use your strengths to glorify God?

    His Response   *Her Response*

_____   _____

_____   _____

_____   _____

_____   _____

_____   _____

_____   _____

3. Describe your weaknesses. How have these weaknesses hurt you in the past? How can you overcome them in the future?

    His Response   *Her Response*

_____   _____

_____   _____

_____   _____

_____   _____

_____   _____

_____   _____

4. The Bible promises a *"way of escape"* (1 Cor. 10:13). How have you overcome temptation in the past? Could you write a prescription for victory to share with others?

His Response   *Her Response*

_____   _____

_____   _____

_____   _____

_____   _____

_____   _____

_____   _____

5. What have you learned from Samson to strengthen your character?

His Response   *Her Response*

_____   _____

_____   _____

_____   _____

_____   _____

_____   _____

_____   _____

_____   _____

Marriage-Strengthening Exercises

Read and discuss a book.

Both of you read a book about someone overcoming a problem or temptation. Discuss the book together. Determine how each of you would approach the problem. If differently, discuss your differences.

Talk about your worst decision.

Somewhere in your marriage the two of you have made a corporate bad decision. (Don't discuss a decision that only one of you made that had a disastrous result.) Talk about your decision. Why did you both make the decision? What do you know now that would change your mind about the decision? How did you rebound from the decision? What have you learned from the decision?

Remember these steps in making decisions.

1. Honestly face the fact that you must make a decision.

    a. Know you have a problem.

    b. Know you must do something.

    c. Know you can solve it.

2. Define the situation.

    a. Don't work on symptoms.

    b. Write the problem (a well-defined problem is half-solved).

3. Gather information.

    a. Write facts about your problem.

    b. Look at causes.

    c. Evaluate assumptions.

4. Develop as many alternate solutions as possible. Evaluate each alternative. (It's important to write out as many solutions as you can.)

5. Choose the best course of action.

   a. To make a decision without the above process is guessing.

   b. Decision making is not thinking up what to do, it's choosing the best solution suggested of all the solutions provided.

   c. In an imperfect world, there is no perfect answer, only the best solution at the time.

6. Make the decision work.

   a. Communicate to those involved.

   b. Constantly evaluate.

   c. Keep focused on your goal.

Chapter 7

David and Bathsheba
LEARNING TO PICK UP THE PIECES

Introduction by Ed and Jo Beth Young
Second Baptist Church, Houston, Texas

We know more about David than any other individual in the Bible, except Jesus Christ. David has the longest biography recorded in the Scripture, and God's Word doesn't pull any punches in recording his strengths and weaknesses. There is no hero in the Bible who is exempt from the truth—even David, to whom God refers as *"a man after His own heart"* (1 Sam. 13:14). David's relationship with Bathsheba began as a rooftop affair and unfolds in a three-act play of crime, cover-up, and confession. It's a sad, dramatic, and tragic story, yet so many of us have made the same mistakes.

The good news is that bad beginnings are not decisive in marriage. Failure is not fatal, nor final. The Scripture says, *"Though your sins are like scarlet, they shall be as white as snow; though they are red like crimson, they shall be as wool"* (Isa. 1:18). Forgiveness is always available—that's the grace of God.

We have seen this biblical truth played out time after time throughout our 40-plus years together serving in churches. Couples start tragically and persevere victoriously. A man and woman whose marriage had ended in divorce began visiting our church. Completely unaware of the other's involvement, both found new life in Jesus Christ. Surprised, they discovered each other again and remarried. God took what was broken and made it whole again. This is the story of redemption. It's a story of reconciliation. As Jesus Christ reconciles us with the Father, He also reconciles us to one another.

Do you want to have a great marriage? Read the following chapter carefully. Pause frequently and reflect on the truths of God's Word. Allow Him to do a wonderful work in your life and in your marriage. If you follow these truths, we guarantee you'll have a love that will last a lifetime.

Learning to Pick up the Pieces

2 Samuel 11:1–12:25

Have you ever seen a couple get married and you thought inwardly, "How long will it last?" When you look at the way David and Bathsheba began—in adultery—you would never expect that they would eventually have a good marriage or that they could ever be used of God. However, their relationship that began in adultery ended with Bathsheba as the last and the most influential wife of David. There are five women mentioned in the genealogy of Jesus in Matthew 1:1-17; Bathsheba is one of them. She eventually had two sons. The first was Solomon (his name means "peace"), and Solomon's line extends to Joseph, the stepfather of Jesus. Her other son was Nathan, whose line extends to Mary, the mother of Jesus. So what began in the shadow of adultery was brought into the light of salvation when the children of David and Bathsheba were ultimately responsible for Jesus, the Messiah.

Counseling Approach

David was a shepherd, a caregiver, and a gentle man who knew how to protect his flock from wild animals. He was a shepherd, knowing where to lead the flock. And he had great attributes for being a great husband.

David knew God as his courage–giver and source of strength in victory over wild predators and giant enemies. Strength, courage, and knowledge of God were David's greatest attributes for being a great husband.

David was a psalmist and loved love music. He wrote music and prayers. His sensitivity and love was often expressed through poetry and music.

David was a king. He had wealth and power along with leadership and understanding of enemy tactics.

But all of these wonderful attributes could also lead to great sin. If he always won, he might get greedy for self–fulfillment. If everyone loved him, they might let him get away with murder. If he always got what he wanted, his power could cause him to sin.

Lust, power, greed, success, and riches can destroy a person if he or she loses sight of where true values lie—in loving a God and fellow man, and in having the utmost respect for covenant.

Why Was David Open to Temptation?

David had spent 13 hard years in the wilderness from his late teens through his late twenties. He was pursued by Saul, driven away from home, and was away from the presence of God in the Tabernacle. When David first became king, he had a number of difficult military campaigns, also away from his home. Now that David was middle-aged, perhaps he thought he could take it easy and enjoy the fruit of his accomplishments.

What Did David Do to Contribute to His Fall?

Several circumstances led to David's infidelity. It happened in the springtime, when there is a new surge of life—*"at the time when kings go out to battle"* (2 Sam. 11:1). Men and women naturally seem to think of love more during spring than any other time of year.

A second circumstance suggests that David evaded his responsibility—*"David remained at Jerusalem"* (2 Sam. 11: 1). When he should have been with his warriors in the field, David stayed in Jerusalem where it was comfortable.

Then there was a third circumstance. David couldn't sleep, so he *"arose from his bed and walked on the roof"* (2 Sam 11:2). David became sort of a Peeping Tom. He saw a woman bathing and couldn't look away. Once he saw, he kept looking.

In Hebrews 4:15, who is our role model when we are tempted?

_____

_____

_____

_____

_____

How did Jesus overcome temptation? Look in Matthew 4:1-10.

_____

_____

_____

_____

_____

How Did Bathsheba Contribute to the Fall?

While it may appear that Bathsheba was completely innocent and was the victim in this circumstance, there are things that Bathsheba could have done to change the consequences. First, Bathsheba disrobed and bathed on an open rooftop, which was immodest and indecent. When a woman suggestively reveals her anatomy to a man, even unintentionally, she makes it nearly impossible for that man to control his thought life.

Loneliness might have been the second circumstance. Her husband was off to war. Perhaps she wanted companionship. When the messenger came saying that the king wanted to see her, it probably answered a longing for companionship in her heart. After all, David was handsome and compelling.

What Should David Have Done?

Obviously, there are several steps David could have taken to prevent the tragedy. First and foremost, he could have stopped looking at Bathsheba when she was bathing. However, some men have said that even after they turn away, they can't turn off their imaginations. The Bible says, *"Flee sexual immorality"* (1 Cor. 6:18). David could also have immediately gone to Rabbah to be with his troops, which is where he should have been in the first place. Or David could have gone back to his room to write another psalm. After all, when he was disquieted, upset, or discouraged, he wrote psalms to express his deep distress. Why not pen a psalm to express the lust he felt in his body and how to overcome temptation?

We are not responsible for temptation that comes to our door, but we are responsible if we invite it in.

— Martin Luther

What inner secret do we have to help us overcome temptation? Look in Psalm 119:11.

_____

_____

_____

_____

_____

_____

What Should Bathsheba Have Done?

Obviously, she should have bathed indoors, out of public view. When the invitation came from the king, she also could have refused to go. It may be difficult to refuse a king, but Bathsheba should have resolved to be faithful to her husband and remain at home.

According to James 4:7, what should be our outer response
to overcome temptation?

\

\

\

\

How Did David Sin?

The Bible suggests that he did not innocently back into the affair, but he sinned aggressively with his eyes wide open: *"David sent messengers, and took her"* (2 Sam. 11:4). This was a reckless move, for the messengers would have probably returned to their quarters to tell the other servants. What David did wrong was probably known throughout the palace, and he was probably aware that all the servants knew everything. Therefore, when David sent for Bathsheba, he moved from a casual observer to consensual sin, and then to compulsive addiction.

Many affairs begin with a *casual observation*—seeing something or having an innocent discussion about things that shouldn't be approached. Then curiosity or lust kicks in which drives the person to become part of the *consensual sin*. After the affair begins, one or both of the parties can't break it off. It becomes a *compulsive addiction*.

I see her.

Casual observer – I want her.

Consensual sin – I will have her.

Compulsive addiction – I can't break it off.

What Was the Result of this Tryst?

David might have thought this was a one-night stand to satisfy his lust. But in the providence of God, Bathsheba later sent word that she was pregnant. Now he was faced with a worse dilemma.

How does sin get into our thinking and life? Read James 4:17.

_____

_____

_____

_____

_____

David thought through the ramifications and knew his leadership would be severely questioned when people found out he had committed adultery with Bathsheba. After all, he was the king, and the seventh commandment said, *"You shall not commit adultery."*

How Did David Try to Cover up?

First, David brought Uriah home under the pretense that he had business for him. But when Uriah arrived in Jerusalem, he stayed in the soldiers' quarters next to the palace. He did not go to his wife, so he did not have sexual relations with her. Uriah probably stayed next to the king's palace, thinking David may have a task for him. Or perhaps he just wanted to be ready when David sent him back to battle.

When David realized his plan didn't work, the next night he threw a big party to get Uriah drunk. David was now compounding his sin because the Bible says, *"Woe to him who gives drink to his neighbor"* (Hab. 2:15). But even in his drunkenness, Uriah was too loyal to go sleep at home with his wife. Again, he stayed in the soldiers' quarters.

> *If we hide our sin, God reveals it. If we acknowledge our sin, God forgives it.*

As a last resort, David sent a note back to Joab in care of Uriah. In the note, David instructed Uriah to be placed in the hottest battle, then for all other soldiers to retreat, leaving Uriah to die. Little did Uriah know that the message in his hand was his own death warrant.

Uriah was involved in a severe battle and when the other soldiers retreated, he was killed. It might as well have been David's own hand on the sword that killed Uriah.

According to Second Samuel 11:27, when the message reached David that Uriah was dead, what did David do?

_____

_____

_____

_____

David thought he had hidden his sin. He thought no one would know. After all, sometimes children are born early, while others come late. As far as David was concerned, everyone would think the baby born to Bathsheba was legally his, when in fact, it was immorally his.

What Was God's Response?

How is it that we think we can hide things from God? Because God is omniscient, He is all-knowing. And because God is omnipresent, He is present everywhere at the same time. Therefore, God knew what David had done. The king had hidden his sin from everyone but God. *"The thing David had done displeased the Lord"* (2 Sam. 11:27).

How Did God Deal With the Situation?

The king who was supposed to lead the nation in righteousness had committed adultery. God could have dealt with it privately to replace David from the throne, but that wasn't God's way.

"Against You, You only, have I sinned, and done this evil in Your sight. Hide Your from my sins, and blot out all my iniquities. Create in me a clean heart, O God, and renew a steadfast spirit within me. Do not cast me away from Your presence, and do not take Your Holy Spirit from me" (Psalm 51:4,9-11).

God sent the prophet Nathan to tell David that he had sinned. Nathan probably had a difficult time with this assignment. If David had killed Uriah, wouldn't David consider killing him? Since David had gone to elaborate plans to cover up his sin, wouldn't the king eliminate Nathan to keep the sin covered? Nathan "preached" a parable to bring conviction to the king:

Two men lived in a certain town; one was rich and the other was poor.

The rich man owned many sheep and cattle, but the poor man only owned one lamb. The small ewe lamb was the delight of the poor man—it played with his children, ate from his plate, and drank from his cup.

The poor man loved the little lamb so much that he would hold it in his arms like a little baby daughter.

A stranger traveling through the area was invited to stay at the home of the rich man. But instead of killing one of his lambs, the rich man took the poor man's lamb, killed it, and served it to the stranger.

What Was David's Response?

David had been a shepherd and probably had a small ewe lamb much like the one described in the parable. When David heard the story, he was furious, as any shepherd would be. But he wasn't angry because he thought Nathan knew his secret; David was furious because of the injustice done to the poor man. And he was doubly furious because the one sheep had been taken.

When David heard the parable from Nathan, what did he say? Look in 2 Samuel 12:5-6.

_____

_____

_____

_____

Little did David know that his rash response in judgment was the punishment he had leveled for himself.

The prophet Nathan wasn't intimidated by King David. He was on business for the Lord, who was his real King. Nathan pointed his finger at David and announced, "You are the man!" In an instant, David realized that the entire plot was known. Immediately, he realized that God knew what he had done, and in conviction, David yielded to the Lord. Nathan asked, *"Why have you despised the commandment of the Lord, to do evil in His sight?"* (2 Sam. 12:9).

Before leaving the room, Nathan said David would be judged by his own verdict. There would be a fourfold punishment on David.

David's Fourfold Punishment

1. Murder: *"The sword shall never depart from your house"* (2 Sam. 12:10). Eventually Absalom, David's prize son, would kill another of his sons, Amnon.

2. Rape: *"I will raise up adversity against you from your own house"* (2 Sam. 12:11). Amnon would rape Tamar.

3. Humiliation: *"I will take your wives before your eyes and give them to your neighbor"* (2 Sam. 12:11).

4. Death: *"The child who is born to you shall surely die"* (2 Sam. 12:14).

David was overwhelmed with conviction. For the next seven days he fasted before God, pleading for the life of the child. It was David's sin, not the sin of the child—the baby was innocent. Psalm 51 reflects the deep remorse of David as he wept and pled for the life of the child.

What You Must Do

Confess it.
Forsake it.
Leave it in the past.

This sin was so great that a hundred years later when the writer was listing the genealogy of the kings of Israel and mentioned the greatness of David, he could not forget his sin: *"except in the matter of Uriah the Hittite"* (1 Kings 15:5).

What Is Necessary After a Couple Sins?

A couple who begins a relationship in sin should do the same thing as David. There is a threefold step in dealing with sin. First, you must confess it.

What does First John 1:9 say about the confession of sins?

_____

_____

_____

_____

But just confessing (saying the same thing) is not enough. There is a second step: You must forsake your sin. This is called *repentance*. Even if a couple has lived together, the man and woman must separate until the marriage becomes legal. If you want God's forgiveness, you must be willing to live by God's ordinance after you have confessed the sin.

Finally, there is a third step. You must leave it in the past. If God has forgiven your sin, then don't wallow in the mire of self-pity. Don't continue rolling in the mud of self-condemnation. When the sin has been cleansed, get up and walk away daily in closer fellowship with God.

Forgiveness is so important in marriage. Anytime a couple sins, whether it is a sin before or after the marriage, they must learn to walk in God's forgiveness. When we confess our sins to God and repent of them, the Bible says we are cleansed and forgiven. That means that if God says you are clean, you should now act in a clean way. Those who refuse to accept God's forgiveness are acting in unbelief. Remember, the sin of unbelief is just as terrible as the sin of adultery.

What is God's promise to you when you are tempted?
See First Corinthians 10:13.

_____

_____

_____

_____

After you have accepted God's forgiveness, you must forgive each other. A marriage can never be strong when one mate blames the other for anything they have done wrong.

If God has forgiven you, walk with courage. Yes, there may be rumors and gossip. But your responsibility is to God, not to those who are talking. You can go to them and ask their forgiveness, but if they refuse to forgive you, then there's nothing more you can do.

What is God's reward for those who successfully overcome temptation? Look in James 1:12 for the answer.

_____

_____

_____

_____

How Did Good Come From Wrong?

David did the right thing when he brought Bathsheba into his house and made her his wife. As we have said before in this book, God does not condone multiple marriages. God's standard is one man for one woman, for one lifetime. David was a man after God's own heart, but still he had multiple wives, in part because he was influenced by the culture of his day. The Bible *describes* accurately what happened, but when it indicates that David had more than one wife, that doesn't mean the Bible *prescribes* polygamy for today.

Bathsheba was David's last wife, as well as the most prominent and influential. When Adonijah tried to steal the throne from David to become the next king, it was the wisdom of Bathsheba working with Nathan the prophet that led to Solomon's place on the throne.

What You Must Do

Seek God's forgiveness.
Forgive each other.
Forgive yourself.

The child conceived out of wedlock did die. Why would God cause the suffering of a child, even though it was David who sinned? In God's economy and wisdom, we don't always understand His plan and purpose. In this case, the sin of David was so great that it not only impacted his life but also the lives of his children.

After the baby died, Bathsheba conceived again and Solomon was born. He was given the name Jedidiah, which means "beloved of the Lord." God loved Solomon and had a great plan for him. He was also given the name that means "peace." And while David was a man of war to establish the kingdom, Solomon was a man of peace who reigned over the kingdom.

God elevated Bathsheba to a place of prominence in the Messianic line. Through her son Solomon came Joseph, who became the stepfather of Jesus Christ, Messiah to the world. And through the line of Bathsheba's son Nathan (she named her boy after the prophet who brought conviction of their sin) was born Mary, the mother of Jesus.

> *Man looks at the outward appearance, but the Lord looks at the heart* (1 Samuel 16:7).

Practical Take-Aways

Both David and Bathsheba knew better.

Often, we want to excuse sin by saying, "It's not so bad." Or we want to excuse ourselves by saying, "I didn't realize." But David and Bathsheba knew the commandments of God, including the one that said, *"You shall not commit adultery"* (Exod. 20:14).

Their sin wasn't just against their marriage partner—it was against God.

Both David and Bathsheba did everything possible to save themselves embarrassment and trouble. If God hadn't brought the sin to light, no one would have been the wiser. But God knew, and He cared. This wasn't just a sin against the Ten Commandments; this was a sin against God. David knew this when he prayed, *"Against You, You only, have I sinned"* (Ps. 51:4).

It's possible to do right, even after a bad beginning.

> *Let the words of my mouth and the meditation of my heart be acceptable in Your sight, O Lord, my strength and my Redeemer*
>
> *(Psalm 19:14).*

There have been many couples who have had a rough engagement but have ended up with a good marriage. However, it takes *purpose* to make an *about-face* and go in the right direction. David did that when he brought Bathsheba into his house and took care of the baby. He did that when Bathsheba became the last and most prominent wife. David's prayer of repentance (Psalm 51) indicates his heart was right before God.

Outward circumstances are not enough to keep a person from giving in to temptation.

David had every reason not to sin. He had more than one wife. He was the divine example as king. He knew the Scriptures, and he was a man after God's own heart. All of this, and yet he still sinned. It can happen to any of us. We need to stay close to God and the *"way of escape"* will be given to keep us from falling into temptation (1 Cor. 10:13).

Journaling

Writing your thoughts is a discipline that makes you think clearly about a subject. Since you are serious about developing a strong marriage, use the following questions to guide your thoughts and writings. Remember, writing will clarify your thinking when you write the things you plan to do.

Why Was the Child Taken?

The child was a source of ridicule—*"You have given great occasion to the enemies of the Lord to blaspheme"* (2 Sam. 12:14).

Example:

Lord, we know it's difficult to remain pure in heart and thoughts. We are inundated daily with nudity and temptation on TV, in the movies, and with today's clothing styles. Even unintentionally, our senses are bombarded by outside influences that test and tempt us. Father, let our eyes and thoughts be only for each other just as You intended. Help us to keep our eyes focused on You. We are sorry for our past sins and humbly confess them now to You and to each other. Forgive us, Father, and we will forgive each other. Help us to move forward from this moment on, toward a life of service to each other and to You. Thank you for Your grace and mercy, and for the opportunity to be a good spouse.

1. Write the things you have done to overcome temptation. Include your prayers, your favorite Bible passages, or any other thing that helped you gain victory.

His Response   *Her Response*

_____   _____

_____   _____

_____   _____

_____   _____

_____   _____

_____   _____

2. Try to describe how you felt when you were victorious over sin. What did that feeling do for you? What Bible verses were meaningful to help give you that victorious feeling?

His Response   *Her Response*

_____   _____

_____   _____

_____   _____

_____   _____

_____   _____

3. Can you remember the feelings of despair when you were out of fellowship with God? How did you feel? Revisit these feelings to make sure you won't return to them.

His Response   *Her Response*

_____   _____

_____   _____

_____   _____

_____   _____

Marriage-Strengthening Exercises

Study the Lord's Prayer.

Study the Lord's Prayer to see the role of prayer in delivering one from temptation and evil. Add to your reading list Chapters 9 and 10 of the book *Praying the Lord's Prayer* by Elmer Towns.

Devise a plan of prayer.

Lay out a plan to pray the Lord's Prayer on a regular basis. If possible, pray it out loud together with your mate. Note the petition, *"Lead us not into temptation."* Pray for God to keep both of you from sexual sins.

Choose a mentor.

Pick out an elderly couple who has loved God, each other, and has remained committed to each other throughout life. Study that couple and try to emulate the couple's strong points. If you can get close to the husband and wife, find out their secret of victory. Then follow it.

Chapter 8

Boaz and Ruth
LEARNING TO LOVE AND SUPPORT EACH OTHER

Introduction by John Ed and Lynn Mathison
Frazer Memorial United Methodist Church
Montgomery, Alabama

God is a God who gives second chances. He condemns sin but offers people a new opportunity. He makes new people out of them. He makes them people who are worthy to be respected and gives them opportunities to serve.

Ruth was a Moabitess. She was outside the commonwealth of Israel. But she made a decision that allowed her to live with God's people and enjoy God's economy. God saw the potential in Ruth. In the sovereignty of God, she married Boaz and was in the line of Christ.

We have seen God do the same thing for people in our church. Some people have been far, far away from God but made a decision to follow Christ. God has put them into a wonderful Christian family. He has created special places of service for them. We have seen God take people the world considered failures and make them great leaders.

The story of Ruth is a story of a woman of great character. She was true to her mother-in-law, she was faithful to keep her commitments, and she worked hard. But most importantly, she was faithful in her own integrity. It was that integrity that God created in her that led Boaz to respect her and, consequently, led her to respect Boaz. They were two people from extremely different backgrounds, yet two people whose marriage was built on love that grew out of mutual respect—a couple God used to serve Him in a special way.

Learning to Love and Support Each Other

Ruth 1:16–2:23

Respect is the foundation of love and marriage. Because genuine love always includes giving one's life to someone, it's difficult to love someone without first feeling respect for that person. Ruth respected Boaz's family position and community prestige. She was always careful to honor him and the position he held in the community. At the same time, Boaz respected Ruth's commitment to God, and he often mentioned Ruth's commitment to her mother-in-law. He also respected Ruth for being a hard and industrious worker. There was mutual respect in this marriage.

How does God's Word instruct a wife to show respect for her husband? See First Peter 3:1-4 and Ephesians 5:22.

_____

_____

_____

_____

The Problem

The Book of Ruth begins with a family in the city of Bethlehem grappling with a financial problem. There was a famine in the area and many families didn't have enough to eat. Elimelech and Naomi were respected community members. The term *Ephrata* that described them implies they were "blue–bloods," meaning they were linked to the original settlers of Bethlehem. They had position in the community. But social status isn't worth much when you don't have anything to eat. It was probably at this time when Elimelech lost his house and property to creditors because he couldn't pay his bills.

Counseling Approach

Family backgrounds are very significant in determining what a marriage will be like. There are two histories at work in a marriage. The strengths from both can be assets to the marriage, while understood weaknesses or injuries can indicate where support is needed. Experiences from a previous marriage should only be shared, if at all, with a current spouse in ways which build trust and intimacy.

It's not necessary or even correct to disregard all things from a previous marriage to make a subsequent marriage a success. It is vital, however, that primary respect be had from the present spouse, and that great care be taken if one chooses to speak about any personal history prior to him or her.

Remember the good things from your previous marriage and build on them in the present one. Forget about the negative things and don't repeat them. Nothing says that a married couple must be similar in age. However, if a marriage involves partners of considerably different ages, there will likely be other differences including social habits, levels of activity, or friendship preferences that will need to be accommodated or worked through.

The older mate may have difficulty keeping the same hours. The younger may wish to be far more social and festive. Tolerance and clarity on the part of both is especially important in such cases. A little willingness to enter into new things will also benefit any marriage.

Respect must be a main pillar supporting the marriage. The older mate may possess wisdom from more experience, yet it would be unwise for anyone to imply lesser respect for the younger. The younger mate may have respect for the older due to age, while not respecting the older mate's wisdom and years of learning.

The older mate may want an heir. This would be a good talking point before marriage.

According to First Peter 3:7 and Ephesians 5:28, how does God instruct a husband to care about and respect his wife?

_____

_____

_____

_____

Heat of Trouble Reveals One's Character

While lack of money was a problem, Elimelech had a deeper problem, probably an unseen character flaw that the other members of the community hadn't noticed. When depression hit the community, he didn't stay to fight the problem, nor did he trust God to feed him and his family. Instead, Elimelech planned to cross the Jordan Valley into the well-watered plains of Moab. Because the grass is always greener on the other side of the fence, and since Elimelech could see the green, well-watered fields of Moab from his home in Bethlehem, he thought life would be better there. So Elimelech began making plans to move.

The problem was that Moab was a foreign nation, with a foreign culture and foreign gods. The Bible records, *"A certain man of Bethlehem, Judah, went to dwell in the country of Moab, he and his wife and his two sons.... And they went to the country of Moab and remained there"* (Ruth 1:1-2). There's nothing wrong with a man seeking financial opportunities for his family, but if it means depriving one's family of spiritual nurturing, then it's no blessing.

Two Hebrew words seem to indicate Elimelech's creeping spiritual paralysis. First, the word *dwell* (Ruth 1:1) implies that he intended to live in Moab temporarily. He probably intended to return to the Holy Land after the financial crisis was over. Next, the phrase *remained there* (Ruth 1:2) means they settled there permanently. In time, they were no longer merely living in Moab; rather Moab was living in them. Elimelech's surface troubles with money revealed a deeper problem.

Why Moab Was Wrong

- The family was separated from its spiritual support.

- The family was exposed to an adulterous and evil lifestyle.

- The family was separated from extended family care and influence.

What Happens to Our Faith When Trouble Comes?

When we disregard God in our struggle to make our lives work, we end up deepening our troubles. Elimelech died in Moab, leaving Naomi a widow with two boys in her care. Elimelech's decisions affected his sons, as well, since they predictably married outside of the covenant to Moabite women. The sons then died young, leaving their widows, who had been raised on the pagan worship of Chemosh, with Naomi, who now had no fellowship or support among any covenant people. She thought God was as far away from her as she felt herself to be from Him. But God was not absent.

As when Joseph, the son of Jacob, told his brothers that what they meant for evil, God meant for good, so the suffering produced by Elemilech's costly actions became a kingdom story of redemption. One of Naomi's daughters-in-law reluctantly left Naomi to return to her own family. The other, Ruth, had been witnessed to enough by Naomi's love that she refused to be separated from Naomi and instead devoted herself to serving Naomi and her God, Jehovah.

Naomi looked back across the Jordan Valley to Bethlehem and saw that the famine was over. The fields of Bethlehem were now green, and she made a decision—she decided to return home.

Ruth understood that, because she was a Moabitess, she had little chance of remarrying in Judah. This fact would have been terrifying to a widow alone in those days, but especially so in light of relocating to a strange land just recovering from a ten-year famine. However, Ruth chose the noble path rather than the familiar and its better prospects for survival

Because security is in the eye of the beholder, Our security seems elusive when we don't know the future.

Her beautiful words to Naomi sang out her courage risk of starving with her rather than being separated from her. Ruth knew that alone, Naomi had little chance at her age.

These compelling words so beautifully express devotion and respect that we, Elmer and Ruth, included them in our own marriage vows spoken on August 21, 1953.

How Did Ruth Put Faith in the Lord?

The two of them left Moab for Bethlehem. Ruth was new in her faith to Jehovah, but the Lord responded to the courage of her commitment and its loving motive by blessing her faith and her way. When Ruth entered Bethlehem, the community must have seen her faith because Boaz later said, *"A full reward be given you by the Lord God of Israel, under whose wings you have come for refuge"* (Ruth 2:12). Just as Ruth's new faith was important to her, it was also important to Boaz. The salvation faith of both husband and wife is a necessary foundation for a Christian marriage.

True security is only in finding and following God. Because only He knows the future.

What Did It Cost Ruth to Put Her Faith in Jehovah?

The Lord had given Ruth a strong enough faith to leave her family and heathen gods. This is another thing Boaz respected about her when he said, *"You have left your father and your mother and the land of your birth, and have come to a people whom you did not know before"* (Ruth 2:11).

Entreat me not to leave you, or to turn back from following after you; for wherever you go, I will go; and wherever you lodge, I will lodge; your people shall be my people, and your God, my God. Where you die, I will die, and there will I be buried. The Lord do so to me, and more also, if anything but death parts you and me (Ruth 1:16-17).

What Brings Happiness Today?

Years ago a candidate for Miss America was asked while being interviewed, "What would you like to do in life?" The young girl answered, "To have fun." While there's nothing wrong with having fun, is it the admirable purpose in life? Fun should never be the goal that motivates us. Fun is a byproduct that comes from successfully walking the road of life. Living successfully out of the heart instead of the flesh builds inward happiness, and that contentment inevitably amplifies everything that is fun in life. That same contentment also assures greater comfort when life isn't fun.

What Character Depth Is Visible in Ruth's Life?

Obviously, choosing to leave the familiar security of her homeland was not a purely rational decision. Logic would have compelled the opposite choice. Her heart told her to follow Jehovah, regardless of the circumstances or what others thought. She left her family and her whole background because even though she was raised pagan, she had the integrity to live compassionately and honestly out of her heart. Integrity also gave Ruth the willingness to work hard in the fields to provide food for herself and Naomi. Hard work was a way of life.

One of the most important qualities a young person brings to marriage is *integrity*, which means being honest with oneself. Ruth had integrity, and that was the most valuable thing about her character.

God has blessed our modern world with many comforts and much prosperity that should be appreciated and used for His glory. It seems, though, that our abundance of comfort and security has encouraged the development of more appetite than character. As good as it is for a young person to be physically attracted to someone they intend to marry, character is the real thing—the only thing— that a person truly falls in love with in another.

> *The flesh looks on the outward appearance of the body;*
>
> *A godly heart looks on the inward character of another's heart.*

Lessons That Lead to a Happy Marriage

A loving relationship with parents and siblings prepares one for a happy marriage.

We've all heard the mother-in-law jokes and the fact that a young wife can never cook as well as a young groom's mother. Sometimes friction may develop between a young wife and her mother-in-law because they do things differently. But Ruth's loving relationship to her mother-in-law prepared her for a loving relationship with Boaz.

An unhappy childhood can be overcome.

Nothing is revealed in the narrative about Ruth's early home life. If she had poor role models in her parents, she overcame it. Ruth was strengthened by the love she received from her mother-in-law. Any child who is deeply loved by his or her mother will usually form a strong self-identity. The child who has a healthy relationship with his or her parent will have fewer emotional problems than one who can't get along with their parents. Probably to Naomi's credit, Ruth developed a loving relationship with her mother-in-law and later a loving relationship with her husband.

Developing kindness prepares one for marriage.

When Naomi and Ruth returned to Bethlehem, apparently Naomi was too old to work in the fields. Whether or not that was the case, Ruth was much younger and stronger, so she went out to glean in the fields. That was hard work, stooping, bending all day under a hot sun, gathering, and then thrashing grain. After this, Ruth had to carry it home. Ruth did all this for her mother-in-law—certainly a kind act. Her unselfishness before marriage equipped her for a wonderful marriage.

Separation

Elimelech preferred security over faith in God's protection. Ruth wouldn't stay in a heathen land.

Developing kindness and love begins with the Lord.

Because Jehovah is a loving God, He gives us love for other people. Therefore, it is only appropriate that the greatest commandment deals with love: "You shall love the Lord your God with all your heart"; and when we do that, we gain strength to "love your neighbor as yourself." Ruth's love for other people was enlarged by her love from and for Jehovah.

What Did Boaz Think of Ruth?

Boaz was moved by what he had heard about Ruth. Not only was she loyal to Jehovah, Ruth separated herself from her pagan background and became loyal to her new family. Boaz commented, *"It has been fully reported to me, all that you have done for your mother-in-law since the death of your husband"* (Ruth 2:11).

How did Boaz express his respect for Ruth? How would Boaz use Ruth's example to admonish the young people of this postmodern age? Look in Ruth 2:11-12.

_____

_____

_____

_____

Boaz was apparently an older man. Referring to Ruth as *"my daughter"* (Ruth 3:10) is something that an older man might say to someone who was young enough to in fact be his daughter. Also, the fact that Boaz owned fields, had servants, and was a respected leader in the community who sat at the gates all imply his seniority. It is unlikely, however, that he had yet reached old age by the time he met Ruth, who was probably in her twenties.

How Did Boaz Demonstrate Faith in the Lord?

Acknowledging God in all things was as normal as breathing for Boaz. When he greeted his servants, he said, *"The Lord be with you"* (Ruth 2:4). Later, when he was talking with Ruth, he talked about God: *"Blessed are you of the Lord, my daughter!"* (Ruth 3:10). Later when he made a promise, he based his word on the integrity of God: *"I will perform the duty for you, as the Lord lives!"* (Ruth 3:13)

A husband must be a man of God for the marriage to be heavenly. He has a calling to provide leadership for the spiritual care of the family. Many marriages flounder because husbands are (a) not prepared to lead the family, (b) are unwilling to lead the family, or (c) don't recognize the centrality of spiritual life in a healthy family.

There are countless joys to be experienced in a loving, respectful marriage, many fulfilling challenges, and a lot of just plain fun. The fact that marriage and family are serious business, however, must never escape anyone's awareness. The well-prepared man will be conscious of the kinds of things that can threaten the spiritual life of a family and the health of relationships. But he will keep his eyes and heart fixed upon the Lord, and will have committed himself to continually growing in faith as the chief servant of his home.

How Did Boaz Show Respect for Ruth?

When Boaz first saw Ruth in the fields, he asked, *"Whose young woman is this?"* (Ruth 2:5). His workmen replied that she had asked to glean in the field; *"So she came and has continued from morning until now, though she rested a little in the house"* (Ruth 2:7). Boaz later acknowledged her diligence.

In the Old Testament, there were no welfare checks. Rather, the Lord made provision for the poor and widows, not permitting farmers to reap the corners of their grain fields nor to go back to gather the gleanings (any grain that is dropped by the harvesters). Farmers were to leave this grain for the poor, the foreigners, the widows, and orphans (see Lev. 23:22; Deut. 24:19). By these standards, Ruth and Naomi qualified for God's welfare. But even this system linked rewards to the level of effort in gleaning. Thus, Ruth went to work with the others, gleaning the harvest to take care of her needs.

> *Ruth was made ready for a love relationship with Boaz, because of her healthy relationship with the Lord and her new family.*

While there's nothing wrong with being beautiful and dressing properly, there is more to life than just being a fashion authority. While the Bible commands us to be a good testimony by the way we act and dress, our inner person is more important than the outer appearance. Nowhere does the Bible say that Ruth was outwardly beautiful. She asked the question, *"Why have I found favor in your eyes, that you should take notice of me, since I am a foreigner?"* (Ruth 2:10). Ruth was aware that men noticed women, and she wanted to know why Boaz had noticed her. The answer was found in her quiet, humble spirit, which was one of her greatest assets. This is the quality admonished in the New Testament (see 1 Pet. 5:5).

How Did Boaz Provide for Ruth?

Boaz told his workers to allow Ruth to glean near them, as close as possible. But he went a step further and instructed them from time to time to drop extra grain for Ruth to glean. He also told them to let her cool her thirst. When a man admires a woman, he wants to give her something. Boaz had compassion for Ruth and made extra provisions for her.

What Brought Them Together?

While it looks like circumstances brought them together, it was the hand of God that guided Ruth to the field of Boaz. *"And she happened to come to the part of the field belonging to Boaz, who was of the family of Elimelech"* (Ruth 2:3). This means she just happened to choose the field of Boaz, not knowing he was a distant relative to her deceased father-in-law. What seems to be coincidental in your life many times is the work of God. *"And we know that all things work together for good to those who love God, to those who are the called according to His purpose"* (Rom. 8:28).

How was Ruth Attracted to Boaz?

It is not known if Boaz was a physically attractive man or how affluent he was. What does stand out about him is his gentleness and kindness, attributes that any woman would find attractive.

How Did the Law of God Bring Them Together?

The Old Testament law provided that a childless widow could seek marriage with her late husband's nearest kinsman (usually a brother if one was available and willing) so that their first son could inherit the deceased man's birthright and money. This is called a Levirate marriage (Levirate means "brother").

Apparently, Elimelech had owned property near Bethlehem in Judah, but may have lost it in default on a loan taken during the famine. Probably for the sake of brevity or discretion, Boaz tells the town leaders that Naomi sold the land (see Ruth 4:3). Old Testament law helped protect against permanent loss of birthright, though, by requiring that all property be returned to the eldest male heir of the original family owners on the year of Jubilee, which came every 50 years. So the property that would have eventually been restored to Elimelech's descendants was in danger of being permanently lost since there were no male heirs.

How Did Ruth Approach Boaz?

Out of obvious respect for him, Ruth didn't embarrass Boaz by publicly pressing him to fulfill the noble obligation of Elimelech's kinsman. Nor did she try to entice or coax him into it. With Naomi's advice, she went to him privately when no one else was around. In those days, it would have been difficult for Ruth to arrange an interview with Boaz, so Naomi devised a plan where the two of them could talk.

After the final threshing of a harvest, farmers and workers would celebrate with a feast. Until the grain could be sold or safely stored, the owners would usually sleep near the harvest to protect it from animals and thieves. Naomi knew what the men would do, so she prepared Ruth to go talk with Boaz.

Naomi instructed Ruth to wash, put on her best clothes, and add the best fragrance (perfume). She told Ruth that after Boaz went to sleep with his grain, she should approach him like a servant out of respect and humility. Ruth did not lie with him in an intimate way. Rather, she lay at his feet as a servant might lie at the feet of a master. Since the fall harvest has chilly nights, a servant kept the feet of his master warm. Ruth did what Naomi instructed. In the middle of the night, when Boaz awakened to see that Ruth was there, he was startled at first until Ruth explained and made her request. Boaz was so flattered and appreciative of the respectful and considerate way she entreated him that he was won over instantly.

What should be understood here is that Ruth wasn't using some obscure legal maneuver to win Boaz's heart. Every element of this transaction was foundational to the Law and universally respected without question. This is because property, inheritance, and family birthright were so important and central to the covenants of God. Even though she didn't understand it, Ruth was honoring God's Law when she said to Boaz, *"I am Ruth, your maidservant. Take your maidservant under your wing, for you are a close relative"* (Ruth 3:9). Ruth was telling Boaz two things: First, she is a kinsman, and second, it was a matter of honor for him to redeem her.

> *How did Ruth respect Boaz in words and in the way she entreated him? In what ways, if any, would her character contrast favorably with the level of common respect generally practiced today? See Ruth 2:13 and 3:6-11.*

_____

_____

_____

_____

How Did Boaz Handle the Proposal?

Boaz must have seen how Ruth respected him in the way she approached the situation. And he showed respect to her in return. *"Then he said, 'Blessed are you of the Lord, my daughter! For you have shown more kindness at the end than at the beginning, in that you did not go after young men, whether poor or rich. And now, my daughter, do not fear. I will do for you all that you request, for all the people of my town know that you are a virtuous woman'"* (Ruth 3:10-11).

Boaz, of course, agreed to his levirate duty, but then, unknown to Ruth and Naomi, he decided to be more than just the levirate. Boaz proposed to the elders that the gracious (and Christ-foreshadowing) work of a "kinsman redeemer" was needed on behalf of Naomi. He then cleverly managed to secure the honor of being the one to marry Ruth and then to purchase back (redeem) Naomi's land so she could benefit from it, and so Ruth's son would be assured of inheriting it in Elimelech's name.

The Qualities of Ruth

- Respectful of Boaz

- Requested marriage humbly

- Reputation of integrity

What Did Boaz and Ruth Not Do?

Boaz told her to lie down and sleep until the daytime, knowing there were dangerous animals and threatening men on the road at night. In the darkness of the night, Boaz did not try to take advantage of Ruth, nor did Ruth try to entice Boaz. He protected her. The Bible says she slept at his feet until morning (see Ruth 3:14). Both showed self-control, which comes from a spirit-controlled life. They honored themselves and the Lord with their purity, and that inevitably brought blessing to them. Couples who don't obey God this way may suffer guilt, loss of self-respect, and injury to their lives and hearts that may make adjusting to each other in marriage difficult. A person who cannot wait and show deep respect for each other before marriage may not be worthy of as much trust after marriage as one who prefers purity over gratification.

We live in a society of "free love" where being a virgin is no longer expected before marriage. Many young people experience sex before graduating from high school, and often a boy tells a girl, "If you love me, you'll have sex with me." But this is total deception. Two people having sex outside of marriage are not expressing love for each other. They are really expressing love for themselves, because most sex outside of a marriage commitment is simply self-gratification.

What Was the Result of Their Marriage?

The healthy relationship of Boaz and Ruth before marriage was the foundation for a healthy relationship after marriage. *"So Boaz took Ruth and she became his wife; and when he went in to her, the Lord gave her conception, and she bore a son"* (Ruth 4:13).

But there is still greater significance to this story. The young woman who was outside the covenant of God became faithful to the Lord and entered the ancestral line of the Messiah. Ruth's son, Obed, became the grandfather of King David, continuing the lineage through which Jesus would come. Little did Ruth know when she made a spiritual decision for God that she would be among the most honored of all women in history. All of this because Ruth, a pagan Moabitess, risked possible destruction in self-imposed exile from her own country to sacrificially love a Jewish mother-in-law.

What Happened to the Mother-in-Law?

One might expect that Naomi would drop out of the picture now that Ruth was married to Boaz, because there may have been a new mother-in-law—Boaz's mother. But that didn't happen. When Obed was born to Ruth and Boaz, the women of Bethlehem said to Naomi, *"Blessed be the Lord, who has not left you this day without a close relative; and may his name be famous in Israel! And may he be to you a restorer of life and a nourisher of your old age; for your daughter-in-law, who loves you, who is better to you than seven sons, has borne him"* (Ruth 4:14-15).

According to Ruth 4:13, how did the Lord bless this marriage?

_____

_____

_____

_____

Naomi lived in the home with Ruth and Boaz and became the nursemaid to young Obed. She took care of the young baby as if he was her own child, and Ruth and Boaz happily permitted it. Naomi was so identified with the young baby that the women in the community said, *"There is a son born to Naomi"* (Ruth 4:17). They were rejoicing with Naomi that the birthright and family name of her husband had been redeemed. But they also may have been delighting in the new smile and light on Naomi's face. Besides all of this, they would have also seen spiritual renewal in Naomi. God's mercy upon Naomi undoubtedly energized her faith in and faithfulness to the Lord. Naomi determined to raise Obed to be a godly man.

Practical Take-Aways

Obstacles can be overcome by God's grace.

Ruth demonstrated that even though she faced obstacles, they could be overcome by unhesitating trust in the Lord God. Even when Naomi told Ruth there was no chance of her ever marrying in the Holy Land, Ruth made a decision to follow the Lord. Ruth did not go to the Holy Land seeking another husband. But when she put the Lord first, God answered her needs by providing one of the best available husbands in Bethlehem.

God's unconditional love is the basis for a happy marriage.

Because Ruth experienced God's unconditional love, she could extend it to her future husband. And with it, Boaz led a healthy family to a unique place in the plan and purpose of God.

Journaling

Writing your thoughts is a discipline that makes you think clearly about a subject. Since you are serious about developing a strong marriage, use the following questions to guide your thoughts and writings. Remember, writing will clarify your thinking when you write the things you plan to do.

Example:

Lord, there are so many lessons for us in understanding the lives of Ruth, Naomi, and Boaz. Father, let us be faithful to our parents and our in-laws, and let us give of ourselves so that they may not suffer. Remind us continually to think of others before we think of ourselves. Father, help us to remember how to be pure in our hearts, and forgive us if we failed to be pure before our marriage. Lord, when we are parents and in-laws, please give us the grace to accept our children's spouses, and help us to minister to them and always be a good example of Your wonderful and forgiving love.

1. What were your fears before you got married? Why were they troubling? What would have happened if your fears came true? Did they?

His Response   *Her Response*

_____   _____

_____   _____

_____   _____

_____   _____

2. What did you look forward to most of all before you got married? Why was that appealing to you? Did it come to pass?

His Response   *Her Response*

_____   _____

_____   _____

_____   _____

_____   _____

_____   _____

_____   _____

3. What role did you have for God in your marriage before it happened? Has it come to pass? What has God done for your marriage that you didn't expect?

His Response   *Her Response*

_____   _____

_____   _____

_____   _____

_____   _____

_____   _____

4. What does your mate respect most about you? Have you been surprised at the areas of your life he or she respects?

His Response   *Her Response*

_____   _____

_____   _____

_____   _____

_____   _____

_____   _____

5. In what ways or areas do you wish your mate respected you more? How would Naomi, Ruth, Boaz, and the wisest people you know advise you on how to cultivate more respect from your mate?

His Response

Her Response

_____

_____

_____

_____

_____

_____

_____

_____

_____

_____

Marriage-Strengthening Exercises

Plan a trip.

Plan a trip to your mate's home area. Take time to see the place where your mate went to school, church, played, etc. Try to see the things that influenced his or her life. Try to see the things that made your mate strong in character or purpose.

Spend quality time with your spouse.

Give time to your mate to learn his or her needs and desires. How can a mate know and appreciate his or her partner if these needs are understood? Only when time is taken to appreciate the other will it happen.

Chapter 9

Joseph and Mary
LEARNING TO SHARE UNCONDITIONAL TRUST

Introduction by Jerry and Macel Falwell
Thomas Road Baptist Church
Liberty University, Lynchburg, Virginia

*W*e count it a privilege to introduce the chapter of Joseph and Mary, obviously one of the greatest Bible couples to ever live. We know that Joseph was impeccable in his relationship to Mary, because even when he found out she was pregnant, Joseph was committed to doing the right thing according to the law of Israel. However, when the angel came and told him of the virgin birth and told him what to do, Joseph, in his integrity, obeyed in faith.

And what can we say about Mary? The angel Gabriel called her the "greatest among women." Look into his words:

"Rejoice, highly favored one, the Lord is with you; blessed are you among women!" (Luke 1:28). Then the angel said, *"Mary…you have found favor with God"* (Luke 1:30). God chose the greatest couple on earth to be the first to receive the Lord Jesus Christ.

When we look at this chapter, we see many marvelous principles by which couples today can guide their marriage. We hope that many couples will read and work through this book together, and be guided by the lessons drawn from the various marriages visited.

Elmer taught the lessons in this book in the Pastor's Bible Class at Thomas Road Baptist Church. The people of the church were amazed at the biblical insights they learned about their marriage. As we watched the people listening to those messages, we knew God's touch was on the truth of this book. Now our prayer is that God will use these lessons to strengthen Christian homes all over the nation.

Elmer and Ruth Towns have been members of our church for more than 30 years. It's sad to say, but some Christian couples are very faithful to God but not to their local church. We can say Elmer and Ruth are faithful in their attendance, in tithing, in service, and have supported this ministry in every way possible. We count it a privilege to be fellow ministers with them for Christ and His Kingdom through the ministry of this book.

Learning to Share Unconditional Trust

Matthew 1:18-25; Luke 1:26-45

A good marriage is based on a foundation of trust. A couple must trust each other, as both put their full trust in God. That's easy because the very nature of love demands trust. Both the man and woman trust each other because they believe the other when they hear "I love you." There is no relationship that needs more trust than the marriage relationship. And never was an engagement tested as severely as the one between Joseph and Mary. After each had pledged their love to one another, Joseph had to appear before the elders at the synagogue to announce his engagement to Mary. She was still in her teenage years, an outstanding young girl who was smart, spiritual, and practical yet yielded to do God's will. Everything seemed rosy until the angel Gabriel appeared to her.

According to Luke 1:30-33, what incredible thing did the angel say to Mary?

_____

_____

_____

_____

_____

Just as quickly as Mary heard the announcement from the angel, she had questions: *"'How can this be, since I do not know a man?'"* (Luke 1:34). The angel explained to her that a supernatural experience would happen: *"The Holy Spirit will come upon you, and the power of the Highest will overshadow you; therefore, also, that Holy One who is to be born will be called the Son of God"* (Luke 1:35). This is what we call the Incarnation: "God became flesh."

What privilege do you have because you are a child of God?
Read First John 1:3.

_____

_____

_____

_____

What relationship do you have with the heavenly Father and what personal
assurance can you have from your heavenly Father? Go to Romans 8:15 and
John 17:11 for the answer.

_____

_____

_____

_____

Counseling Approach

What an unusual situation! Angels told Mary the immediate problem (a child would be conceived out of wedlock) but they didn't begin to explain all the implications on her life this child would have.

In every way, her child would be human. That's why *He* "became flesh" and "grew in wisdom and stature." When the angel spoke to each of them, Joseph and Mary both believed God. There were to be no secrets, and yet, under these unique circumstances, how could anyone possibly know how this child would affect their marriage, their lives, and especially, their other family and community relationships?

God wanted His Son to be raised in a family committed to trusting and obeying Him and His Law. What an awesome responsibility Joseph and Mary had! There were responsibilities on both parents to support, protect, teach, and train the child.

As overwhelming as the responsibilities involved in raising any child are, it is hard to imagine how much more sobering it was for the Holy couple to be raising the Son of God.

But God knew their hearts and entrusted the hope of the world to them.

After the explanation to Mary, she had to make a decision whether to resist the will of God or become the mother of the Son of God. Did she immediately think of Joseph? Did she wonder if giving birth to the Son of God would disrupt any of her plans to be married? What about her love for Joseph? After all, he was her beloved.

Examining the story of the virgin birth leads us to the question of trust. Could Mary trust Joseph to do the right thing? Would Joseph believe Mary was telling him the truth when she told him the baby she was carrying was not his? Would they both trust God?

What Was Mary Like?

First, we know that Mary was pure; she is called *"a virgin"* (Luke 1:27). Second, Mary had a sense of God's presence in her life that came from a daily walk of fellowship with God (see Luke 1:28). She was not a giddy teenage girl. Mary thought deeply about the message of the angel: *"But Mary kept all these things and pondered them in her heart"* (Luke 2:19). It has been said, "Gratitude is the least remembered of all virtues and is the acid test of character." Mary was grateful that her sins were forgiven by God: *"My spirit has rejoiced in God my Savior"* (Luke 1:47); *"Behold the maidservant of the Lord! Let it be to me according to your word"* (Luke 1:38). Mary rejoiced that she had been chosen to fulfill what had been referred to as "the maiden's hope" by generations of Hebrew women since Isaiah prophesied the birth of the Messiah. Above this, however, it can be said that Mary was the first person to receive Christ. But after Mary encountered the angel and submitted to become the mother of Jesus, she faced some questions.

When you trust God for answers to your questions about marriage, you have laid a foundation for a good relationship together.

The Integrity Question

Mary had to consider what people would think of her when, obviously, her pregnancy could not be concealed.

What was Mary's question? Find the answer in Luke 1:34.

_____

_____

_____

The Joseph Question

Mary loved Joseph deeply and didn't want to hurt him, so she must have worried, "What will Joseph think?" But beyond hurting his feelings, she had to ask, "Will Joseph attempt to divorce me or have me punished?"

The Reputation Question

There was a great stigma attached to any woman becoming pregnant outside of wedlock. What would her family and community think of her, and what would they think of her son?

The Practical Question

When Mary was told she would become the mother of Jesus, she asked, "How can this be?"

According to Luke 1:35, the angel told her all she needed to know. What was she told?

_____

_____

_____

_____

The Spiritual Question

Mary had only one basic question to answer: "Will you submit to God?" The Lord was asking her to do what would be embarrassing, questionable, and risky. Remember, there is always some risk in submission to God.

How Did Joseph Find Out?

We do not know how Joseph found out Mary was pregnant. We don't know if Mary told him, if someone else told him, or if he learned from observation or circumstances. *"Before they came together, she was found with child of the Holy Spirit"* (Matt. 1:18).

The Role of a New Father

• To protect the family.

• To provide for the family.

• To plan for the family.

What Was Joseph's Response?

The only thing Joseph knew for sure was that he wasn't responsible for Mary's pregnancy.

In Matthew 1:19, what was Joseph's reaction?

_____

_____

_____

_____

_____

Notice what Joseph did *not* do. He did not react emotionally. He did not verbally attack Mary. He did not worry what people would think about him. We see *trust* in Joseph's response.

Why Did Joseph Consider a Private Solution?

There are several reasons why he might have wanted to deal with this problem privately. He might not have known about the angel and the supernatural conception. Or, if Mary had told him the whole story, he could have doubted her explanation concerning the source of her pregnancy and possibly her emotional health. He may have felt unworthy to raise the Son of God. Whatever the reason, we see that Joseph was godly and gracious in his intentions toward Mary.

What Was Joseph's Greatest Act of Trust?

When the angel told Joseph in a dream that the child was going to be the Messiah, he believed what Mary told him, and he trusted God to work out the details, *"He took to him his wife, and did not know her till she had brought forth her firstborn Son. And he called His name JESUS"* (Matt. 1:24-25).

The Foundation of a Good Marriage

- To forsake all others and cleave to each other

- To love for better or worse

- To trust each other until parted by death

How Mary Trusted Jesus

It was not a matter of trust when Mary and Joseph took a long trip from Nazareth to Bethlehem. They had to obey Caesar and return to their hometown for registration to prepare a tax roll. Providentially, Mary gave birth to her firstborn Son when they arrived in Bethlehem. The story is well-known about how the city was crowded with many others who had also returned to register for the tax rolls. As a result, there was no place for them to stay, so they took lodging in the stable of an inn. It was there that the Son of God was born and then witnessed by the shepherds.

How Is Trust Displayed?

- Trust is sharing your innermost thoughts and feelings and being confident that they will never be used against you.

- Trust is knowing you will be loved and accepted, no matter what happens.

- Trust is having no anxiety or jealousy when your mate talks to someone of the opposite sex.

- Trust will make you willingly vulnerable at all times.

- Trust in one another will grow over the years.

- Both God and your mate can ask you the ultimate question: "Do you really trust me?"

Mary Did What Was Necessary

On the eighth day, Mary followed Joseph to the temple to have Jesus circumcised (see Luke 2:21), and on the fortieth day she returned to offer a sacrifice for her purification (see Luke 2:39). These were activities of the law and were carried out by those Jews who were conscientiously obeying God.

Mary's Trust Is Seen in Her Willingness to Settle in a Home Away From Family

Rather than returning to their home in Nazareth, the young family remained for at least a year in Bethlehem, which was almost a hundred miles away.

It was near the end of this time when the wise men came to Bethlehem with gifts for the baby Jesus. But then the angels warned Joseph that Herod would seek to kill Mary's Son (see Matt. 2:13). In a dream, the angel told Joseph to take Mary and the child and flee to Egypt. Note that the angel came to Joseph acknowledging his headship and duty. So Mary had to trust what the angel told Joseph, just as previously Joseph had to trust what the angel told Mary. She obediently went to Egypt, moving even farther away from her family and home.

As Mary carried her child to Egypt, she was exercising perhaps the greatest trust of all. They had to travel over 200 miles across the desert into a foreign environment with a different language and customs to settle down and begin a new life. Mary was completely uprooted, and there was total darkness concerning their future lives.

The Young Family Stayed There Until the Babe Grew into a Young Child

Again, an angel came to Joseph directing the family to return home because those who tried to kill the Messiah were dead. This would have been an easy decision for Mary, for now she was returning home with her family. We can assume she was excited about the return home to Nazareth, but she probably also had reservations. Would their long absence be resented? Who would still be alive to receive them and help them get settled? Would they be criticized for their decisions?

Mary had not only submitted her life to God, she had submitted her life to her husband, trusting him to do what was best for her and the Child.

What Interferes with the Growth of Trust?

- Arbitrarily giving your opinion.

- Proclaiming your own self-will.

- Doing only what is best for you alone.

- Continually lecturing or fixing.

- Seldom listening.

Trust begins long before the marriage ceremony when couples pledge their will to each other. Trust begins when they share their lives and dreams with each other, knowing that they believe in and will support each other. Trust is nurtured when a husband and wife protect each other's interests at all times. Trust is implied when a young man gives a woman a ring or token of his love. And then trust is verified in a wedding ceremony when husband and wife pledge their life, love, and equity to one another. Then, throughout life, trust is strengthened like a muscle as it is used. The more they trust one another, the more perfect it becomes.

Practical Take-Aways

Both the husband and the wife should always look for directions from God.

The trust that Joseph and Mary lived by in their own lives, they continued together in faith by trusting God and trusting each other.

Both should always seek what is best for all.

You will demonstrate your trust in God by always seeking what is best for your family. Even in these individualistic days, you must practice putting the family unit first.

Share private matters only with each other.

Couples who don't share probably don't trust. But look at the opposite; when you can share anything and everything with your mate, it demonstrates confidence in him or her. Additionally, a mate who fails to keep a confidence probably doesn't respect. But when private matters are kept secure, trust grows because personal interests are protected.

Consult the Lord for family decisions.

When you both put God first, it's easy to establish family oneness around the Word of God, prayer, and seeking His will.

Spend time in prayer seeking direction for the family.

Just because you trust your spouse doesn't mean you don't need to trust God as much to guide you and protect you. Both of you must trust God together even more for His guidance.

Search the Word for principles to guide the family.

You must search the Bible together and separately. This must be a continuing practice, not just in times of need or when problems arise.

Wait for the subtle assurance of God's plan.

God can give both of you an inner assurance of His leading. He can give this separately or together, but both will have peace in it. Wait for it!

Wait on God.

When both of you have a sincere and patient desire to do God's will for the family, God will protect you from making grievous mistakes that will harm your family.

Journaling

Writing your thoughts is a discipline that makes you think clearly about a subject. Since you are serious about developing a strong marriage, use the following questions to guide your thoughts and writings. Remember, writing will clarify your thinking when you write the things you plan to do.

Example:

Father, we know how Mary must have trusted You. Even when she suffered the loss of her Son, she must have known that He died for the sins of the world. Lord, we ask that You plant that same trust in our hearts. Please give us the strength and wisdom to trust and follow each other as Mary and Joseph did, through difficult times, as well as good. With You as our Shepherd, we know that our marriage can survive pain, relocation, deaths in our family, financial hardships, and whatever else may come. Thank you, Father, for creating us in your image and giving us the ability to trust, come what may.

1. Describe your feeling of trust as you approach God. Is it like coming to a father? Did you have a father you could trust?

His Response   *Her Response*

_____   _____

_____   _____

_____   _____

_____   _____

_____   _____

2. How does today's lesson give you a new meaning of *Father* in Heaven?

His Response   *Her Response*

_____   _____

_____   _____

_____   _____

_____   _____

_____   _____

3. How does the term *Father* help you understand God? How will you trust Him more? How will you feel about Him?

His Response   *Her Response*

_____   _____

_____   _____

_____   _____

_____   _____

_____   _____

Marriage-Strengthening Exercises

Make and discuss a Family Trust list.

Both of you do a study on "family trust." List all the ways a wife must trust her husband. List all the ways a husband must trust his wife. Then examine yourself. How well are you doing in these areas? Now it's time to share your results with your mate. Let each of you discuss strengths and weaknesses. You may find that what you think is a weakness isn't perceived that way by your mate. This is a good talking point.

Make and discuss a Child Trust list.

Each of you do a study on "child trust." List all the ways a child must trust his or her parents. List all the ways a parent must trust a child. Then examine your ability to trust your children. Now, husband and wife compare your lists. Can you help each other with the trust factor?

Your children will trust their parents at the approximate rate that your parents trusted you. Why? Because our children pick up more of their attitudes from our actions, not just from our words.

While this book is about Bible couples, this is a good place to apply it to the children of the family.

Chapter 10

Zechariah and Elizabeth
Learning to Reflect Companionship

Introduction by Dr. D. James and Anne Kennedy
Coral Ridge Presbyterian Church
Fort Lauderdale, Florida

*I*f we were to search the Scriptures for a better example of role models for our marriage, we couldn't come up with a more ideal pair than Zechariah and Elizabeth. Both were along in years, as we are. Both were deeply involved for most of their lives in the Lord's work, as we have been. And both are pictured in Luke as finishing faithfully the course upon which they had launched in their youth together—which is precisely what we have endeavored to do since we were young.

We would like to tell every married couple in the world about the importance of beginning well if you hope to finish well. God told us in the earliest days of our career together, "I will do better for you than at your beginnings, and you shall know that I am the Lord." We know that to be true in every way—in our marriage, in the growth of our church from 48 members to more than 10,000, in the expansion of our Evangelism Explosion International program which now encircles the globe, in our accredited prep school and seminary, in our radio and television outreach which blankets America, and in a thousand other ways which we cannot begin to list here.

Regardless of what might appear to be "small beginnings," despite every obstacle, every disappointment, every enemy that may be encountered through the passing years, couples in this day especially need to know that if they will trust God as Zechariah and Elizabeth did, and if they will commit themselves without reservation to become one in Christ Jesus, they will find their "finishing years" to be filled with blessings beyond measure.

Learning to Reflect Companionship

Luke 1:5-25, 57-80

The story of Zechariah and Elizabeth takes place in the sunset years of their lives, and like many elderly couples, they had learned contentment and companionship. They enjoyed each other, they looked at life through the same perspective, and they were happy in the service of God.

What happens when people turn 50? The authors were both asked that question when they turned 50 in 1982. Without realizing it, something switches in your heart from on to off. We no longer found ourselves trying to impress people by making a statement with our lives. People had to take us as we were. We no longer found ourselves striving to prove ourselves or be more than we were. The most appropriate word to describe our lives when we turned 50 was comfortable. We were comfortable with who we were and what God was doing in our lives. Life is like climbing a mountain. Life after 50 is a more comfortable ride. You're comfortable with yourself, your setting, your home, your job, and you're even comfortable with the things you've learned and the attitudes you've acquired.

According to First Chronicles 29:11, what should be the concluding prayer of our life? And for what should we pray?

_____

_____

_____

_____

_____

_____

_____

We have all known couples who have been married for a long time and seem to know each other so well that arguments are few. They have learned over the years how to react to each other, how to plant seeds for thought, and what issues are important to stand firm upon. Their dreams and goals have meshed together in a workable pattern, becoming satisfying and, again, comfortable.

Zechariah and Elizabeth had become comfortable with one another. They served the Lord together as a team. Zechariah faithfully served in the temple while Elizabeth was faithful at home. They personified the spirit of marriage the Lord intended in the garden when He brought Adam and Eve together: *"Therefore a man shall leave his father and mother and be joined to his wife, and they shall become one flesh"* (Gen. 2:24). Zechariah and Elizabeth were one.

While we must not glean too much from what the Bible is silent about, there is no occasion recorded that told of them disagreeing or fussing. Conversely, their visible faith in the Lord and personal communion with Him no doubt cultivated generous, loving hearts for each other and much warmth. Companionship in marriage leads to calmness in one's lifestyle.

Counseling Approach

If you knew ahead of time that you would live happily ever after, you would probably not work on your marriage to make it better, nor would you learn from your mistakes. After all, "happily ever after" is a goal of all marriages. But you never know ahead of time what will happen; so do everything you can to make your marriage the best it can be.

There's a better goal than striving to one day be happy. The best goal is finding companionship each day. Companionship does take time.

Becoming so aware of the other person in thought, goals, likes, and dislikes takes time. Dreams and goals must be worked out together. A life of intimate companionship is satisfying and will bring great comfort to your lives.

Contentment is indeed good—on the other hand, if one settles back, content to rest on the past, it's hard to be ready for God's blessings and God's surprises. He doesn't always fulfill dreams and visions immediately in our lives. Sometimes miracles are finally given birth after many years of faithfulness following their conception.

A Threat to Contentment

Even though it appeared that the marriage of Zechariah and Elizabeth was calm, there was one small dark cloud over them.

According to Luke 1:7, what was the problem?

_____

_____

_____

_____

_____

_____

_____

_____

_____

_____

Characteristics of a Long Marriage

- Companionship: They prefer one another to all others.

- Calmness: They don't lose control of emotions.

- Contentment: They accept and trust God's will.

- Commitment: Their hearts are united, even when their minds aren't.

In those days, being childless was very undesirable and often met with the stigma of doubt about a marriage's favor with God. It was central in importance to a covenant-keeping family. This is because children were an inheritance of the Lord. It may have even cast doubt within the priesthood about Zechariah and his fitness for ministry in the temple. After all, a man had to rule his family well to be a priest, and Zechariah only had a marriage, not a family.

How Did They Handle the Problem?

Even though Zechariah and Elizabeth had no children, they seemed to patiently accept it. There is no record that Zechariah ever blamed his wife. As a matter of fact, he kept on serving God as though the problem did not exist. We, too, can *keep on serving God confidently despite problems, not letting them stop us.* There will never be a perfect time to serve God in our imperfect world. And if you wait until all problems go away before you serve God, you'll never serve Him.

Zechariah showed himself not only fit but also highly desirable for service in the temple. He didn't quit on his marriage. There is indication in rabbinical literature that some priests divorced their wives to marry younger women who could bear children. But that didn't happen here.

What Should a Couple Do When Problems Come?

While there is no perfect answer, there are general principles that can help lead a couple through troubled water.

1. They should pray together that God would give them wisdom.

2. They should search the Word for principles on how to solve or live peacefully with the problem.

3. They should continually encourage one another in the faith and in their love for one another.

4. They should recommit to be steadfast in the ministry the Lord has given them, and in the life they have together.

5. They should wait patiently for God's answer and direction in the matter.

6. They should always be a witness of God's goodness and strength when and however He answers.

According to Matthew 6:33, what should our attitude be toward God and toward this life?

_____

_____

_____

_____

_____

_____

One Life-Changing Day

Most couples can look back on their lives to find one day that was like a fork in the road. Some have had more than one decisive day that changed their destiny. Some couples have had an incredible day of blessing, other couples have had their lives shattered in one day. There can be promotions, layoffs, a discovery of cancer, or a financial windfall. One day can bring to fruition a move to a new city, a birth, or an incredible achievement.

When we are not sure of the future, what should be our attitude?
Go to Romans 4:18 for the answer.

_____

_____

_____

_____

_____

In one life-changing day the entire ministry of Zechariah and Elizabeth was sealed into historical and cosmic significance forever.

What Was Special About That Day?

Zechariah was given the rare honor to burn incense and offer prayers for one week in the holy room of the temple. Jewish antiquities reveal that no priest was chosen for this honor twice in his life, and because of their numbers, most were never so honored.

What should be our response when God gives us a task? Look in Hebrews
11:6 for the answer.

God chose the just and faithful Zechariah for this service and for this particular time when He would echo the former promise He made to Abraham in his old age. It was during this service in the Holy Place that the archangel Gabriel was sent to herald the answer to Zechariah's prayers. Elizabeth would bare him a son who, among the sons of men, there would be no equal.

Why Did God Promise Zechariah a Son?

Even after he was too old to have children, it appears that Zechariah kept asking for a son. The angel reminded Zechariah, *"Your prayer is heard; and your wife Elizabeth will bear you a son"* (Luke 1:13). The original language suggested that they had been praying constantly and continually for a son. What father doesn't want a son to carry on his name and the family line? What father in ministry doesn't want a son to serve the Lord and carry on his ministry?

Why Did God Strike Zechariah Dumb?

This seems like a cruel response on the surface. God gave him the best news he could ever conceive and then took away his ability to laugh, cry, or shout for joy. Not only could Zechariah not respond, he couldn't even whisper the good news in his wife's ear, nor could he share it with a friend over a meal.

According to Luke 1:20, why was Zechariah's power of speech taken from him?

_____

_____

_____

_____

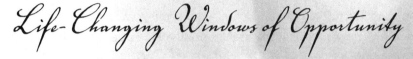

- First-time window of opportunity.

- Once-in-a-lifetime window of opportunity.

- Last-time window of opportunity.

What Did Zechariah Learn From This Experience?

Every time God works in our lives, we should learn a lesson. In this experience, Zechariah learned firsthand about God's great power—God can do anything. Second, Zechariah learned greater humility. Even though he had faithfully prayed for a son over the years, when the miracle finally came, he recognized that it was not out of his worthiness that he was receiving it. In the third place, his faith was strengthened. When the son was finally born, Zechariah obeyed God explicitly. The neighbors pressed for the new baby boy to be named after him—an honor to any father—but Zechariah obeyed God and called the baby John.

What Is Usually Behind Complaints in Marriage?

Just as Zechariah expressed his doubt in a complaint, today many couples express their unbelief with complaints. Some might say, "My spouse will never change."

Others complain that they will never get out of debt. People grumble that things will never get better. We need to remember the simple truth that the angel said about the conception of Elizabeth: *"For with God nothing will be impossible"* (Luke 1:37). Look beyond natural circumstances to the power of God, who can do anything. The same is true with financial problems or any other circumstances that appear unalterable to the flesh. God can do anything He desires. Just remember that true faith pleases God and factors greatly in answered prayers.

Why Did Mary Visit Elizabeth?

The angel who appeared to Zechariah also told Mary that she would conceive the Son of God in her womb. The angel then encouraged Mary with the news that her relative, Elizabeth, had conceived a son. It was only natural that Mary would travel from her home in Nazareth to stay for a while with Elizabeth. Maybe young Mary didn't want her pregnancy revealed, or maybe she wanted to learn from Elizabeth.

When Mary first greeted Elizabeth, Elizabeth clutched her stomach and said an amazing thing. According to Luke 1:44, what did she say to Mary?

Why Did Zechariah Doubt?

• Incredible: It was too good to be true.

• Pain: It was too hard on his wife.

• Unbelief: It was too difficult to accept since the day of miracles had passed.

Then Elizabeth made her great pronouncement: *"Blessed are you among women, and blessed is the fruit of your womb! But why is this granted to me, that the mother of my Lord should come to me?"* (Luke 1:42-43). Notice the spiritual perception of Elizabeth in that statement. Elizabeth's years of faith were brought into focus. Elizabeth understood who Mary's child was and rejoiced that young Mary was counted worthy of the ultimate honor. Young Mary had the privilege all Jewish women dreamed of—to be the mother of God's promised Deliverer. There was no jealousy on the part of the older woman; she rejoiced with the younger Mary.

The Conclusion of Contentment

Eight days after a Jewish boy is born, he is circumcised. It is at this time that the name of the child is confirmed. Many times this becomes a big family event; usually a feast is provided for the family to celebrate the birth of a boy.

Why Did the Neighbors Want to Name Zechariah's Child After Him?

They had probably not been told about the experience with the angel since Zechariah couldn't talk. They hadn't been told that God had prenamed the child John. They knew the conception was highly unusual, for they had only heard in legends of people this old having babies. It would have been customary to call the boy Zechariah after his father since the child was born into the tribe of Levi and would probably go into the temple ministry. The neighbors were only trying to honor the boy's father and preserve tradition.

Why Did Elizabeth Resist?

When the neighbors wanted to call the boy Zechariah, Elizabeth said no, that his name was John. Even though Elizabeth's firm response was full of the Holy Spirit, she would not likely have spoken it without confirmation from her husband. Though Zechariah couldn't speak, somehow the parents were in agreement beforehand. But for the circumcision to proceed, Zechariah would have to write out instructions to call the boy John.

Another Miracle for Zechariah!

In an act of faith and obedience, the elderly father wrote, *"His name is John"* (Luke 1:63). Immediately, God opened his mouth so he could speak, and everyone marveled and wondered what this could mean concerning the child. Zechariah obeyed God, the miracle occurred, and the promise was fulfilled. The Holy Spirit filled Zechariah's heart to speak. The rejoicing words of the Father's work of salvation for His people are now called the Benedictus. Zechariah's lengthy praises suggest that the Lord had been schooling his heart and mind all during his silence.

What Was the Size of This Miracle?

For years Zechariah and Elizabeth longed for a son. Now God exceeded abundantly above their desire. Zechariah had asked for a son to follow him in ministry, but God lifted the answer to a higher level.

According to Luke 7:28, what did Jesus say regarding John the Baptist?

_____

_____

_____

_____

_____

_____

Zechariah's son would be the greatest man ever born. His son would announce to the world the coming Messiah.

Practical Take-Aways

Being comfortable in an uncomfortable world.

Most people don't like change, displacement, transition, and especially the anxiety that comes with a dangerous, unexpected threat. However, the Christian is exhorted to be confident in God at all times and in all circumstances because God is good above all, and He has a perfect plan for us to fulfill. The daily objective for God's people is to abide in Christ (see John 14:20) and the *"peace of God, which surpasses all understanding, will guard your hearts and minds through Christ Jesus"* (Phil. 4:7).

Accept the unexpected as a call to faith.

One day, everything changed for Zechariah and Elizabeth. Their dream would be fulfilled. But because of their advanced age, it was totally unexpected. When God drops the unexpected in your lap, just accept it like Zechariah and Elizabeth. Your greatest work for God can come when you least expect it. Your greatest work of faith may be just around the corner.

Embrace the future.

You never get too old to have a future because it is in future challenges where God delights to reveal Himself. It won't usually be about the past. People retire when they have nothing to do. And young people might as well retire if they have no higher purpose in life. Zechariah thought he was finishing his life's work, but he didn't know his greatest task for God lay in the future raising of his son to be a great prophet. He had to prepare his son to become John the Baptist and prepare the way for Jesus Christ.

Let your children stand on your shoulders to reach higher.

Don't teach your children to just follow in your footsteps. Teach your children to stand on your shoulders and reach higher than you reached. Encourage a desire in them to reach for the stars. Zechariah was greatly used of God as a priest. The Bible describes him as *"righteous before God, walking in all the commandments and ordinances of the Lord blameless"* (Luke 1:6). That's better than good; that's great! It would be very hard for anyone to live a more righteous life than Zechariah. But his son John was even better. That means John the Baptist was greater than Abraham, Moses, David, and the prophets. Zechariah had his greatest calling after he was old enough to retire.

Journaling

Writing your thoughts is a discipline that makes you think clearly about a subject. Since you are serious about developing a strong marriage, use the following questions to guide your thoughts and writings. Remember, writing will clarify your thinking when you write the things you plan to do.

Example:

Lord, we've been talking about becoming comfortable in our companionship. We'd like to find that intimacy with You. It takes quiet listening time on our part, doesn't it? We want to live so closely to You that we'll hear Your voice above all others. Please show us that age still bears fruit. We want our efforts as a couple to bear much fruit.

1. What are the lessons you've learned about contentment while studying this chapter? What does comfortable feel like?

His Response   *Her Response*

_____   _____

_____   _____

_____   _____

_____   _____

2. At what times during your life have you felt most comfortable? Why?

His Response   *Her Response*

_____   _____

_____   _____

_____   _____

_____   _____

_____   _____

_____   _____

3. Are you one who is always planning for the future but never living in the present? What will it take to get you comfortable? How will you know when to turn your attention from the future to the present?

His Response   *Her Response*

_____   _____

_____   _____

_____   _____

_____   _____

_____   _____

_____   _____

4. Zechariah and Elizabeth had to plan for another life after finishing their "first" life. How would you have felt? What would you do?

His Response　　　　　　　*Her Response*

_____　　_____

_____　　_____

_____　　_____

_____　　_____

_____　　_____

Marriage-Strengthening Exercises

Keep dating.

Keep dating all through your marriage! Never get over the good times you have together. Enjoy that comfortable experience. Sometimes your social comfortableness can lead to spiritual comfortableness. If you are comfortable with the Lord, it'll show in life. Your mate will see it, and eventually you'll influence them. So keep seeking those times when you're comfortable with each other.

Make a greater effort on special occasions.

Don't take your mate for granted. You'll keep him or her happy the way you originally made him or her happy. Keep sending the cards and flowers, and don't forget gifts—Christmas gifts, anniversary gifts, Valentine's Day, special remembrances. When the desire for physical sex declines, don't forget the need for inner reassurance is greater. Use every occasion to tell your special soul mate that he or she is special.

Chapter 11

Ananias and Sapphira
LEARNING TO BE HONEST WITH GOD AND EACH OTHER

Introduction by Neil T. and Joanne Anderson
Freedom in Christ, Carefree, Arizona

Elmer and Ruth are our friends, and Neil had the privilege to coauthor *Rivers of Revival* with Elmer. We've had lunch together numerous times and love to share with one another what God is doing in our lives. So we count it a privilege to write this introduction for our dear friends.

People all over the world are living in bondage to the lies they believe. Jesus said the truth will set us free, but the father of lies has infiltrated our ranks and has effectively deceived the whole world (see Rev. 12:9). Consequently, the whole world lies in the power of the evil one (see 1 John 5:19). The Lord knew what the primary battle was, so He had to send a powerful message to the early church. His judgment seems rather severe for the crime, but it was necessary if the Church was going to survive.

Why did satan fill the hearts of Ananias and Sapphira to lie? Elmer correctly points out that their hearts weren't right with God. As a couple, they had agreed together to lie and it cost them their lives. Consequences of lying to one another in marriage may not bear the immediate consequences that Ananias and Sapphira suffered, but they will come. Marriages are being torn apart because one or both will not walk in the light and speak the truth with one another. Intimacy and oneness in marriage are based on trust. If we can't believe one another, we can't trust one another. If caught in a lie, we can choose to forgive one another, but once trust is lost, it is hard to be regained.

Paul said, *"Therefore, putting away lying, 'Let each one of you speak truth with his neighbor,' for we are members of one another. 'Be angry, and do not sin': do not let the sun go down on your wrath, nor give place to the devil"* (Eph. 4:25-27). Such verbal and emotional honesty is what keeps marriages together and the enemy at bay. May the good Lord enable you to put Paul's words into practice in your marriage.

Learning to Be Honest With God and Each Other

Acts 5:1-11

Ananias and Sapphira lived in what many believe was the greatest church of all time, and they lived in this church when it was experiencing its greatest victories. Never again would there be the unity in a local congregation that was evident in the early Jerusalem church: *"They were all with one accord in one place"* (Acts 2:1), and they shared and *"had all things in common"* (Acts 2:44). The church had its greatest power in preaching. Three thousand people had been saved on the day of Pentecost, and a little while later, 5,000 were added to the Church (see Acts 4:4). Many of those in the church had seen the physical Jesus, and now they were living in the power of the indwelling Holy Spirit. What a great day to live and what a great city in which to minister! You couldn't find a better place or church to raise your family. Ananias and Sapphira, who were members of this church, had everything but threw it all away.

In today's legal environment, if a wife plans a crime with her husband but doesn't carry it out, she is a "co-conspirator." Some may think she is only guilty of cover-up, but according to the law, she is just as guilty of the actual crime as he. Those who drive the getaway car from a robbery are just as guilty as those who point the gun and steal the money. In this story, Ananias and Sapphira are both equally guilty of a sin against God.

Counseling Approach

Be careful...in the midst of a great moving of God, satan unleashes all of his hatred and vengeance against God by severely attacking God's most faithful servants. Ananias and Sapphira had everything going for them—reputation and great names to live up to. But their riches did them in because they weren't wise.

> They could have caused the whole church to suffer—they were role models, but they failed.
>
> Be careful...satan is powerful and can cause you to conspire together to sin. What does God say about the wages of sin?

What Did Ananias and Sapphira Have Going for Them?

They not only lived in a great church environment, each of them had the forgiveness of sins that comes from knowing Jesus Christ as Savior. Probably because of their nearness in time to the crucifixion of Jesus, they may have actually heard Him preach.

But they had something else going for them: their parents raised them under the influence of Jehovah. She was given the name Sapphira, which means "beautiful and pleasant;" Ananias was given the name that means "Jehovah is gracious." Their parents had given them special names to indicate their commitment to the Lord.

Ananias and Sapphira not only lived in a spiritually prosperous church, they were financially prosperous as well. The Bible indicates that they had a possession at least worth enough to get the attention of the church. When they brought the money they reportedly got from selling it, most people knew about it.

And beyond all this, the couple was accepted by the Jerusalem church so that they had access into its daily operations. They could come and go among church leaders—something not all members could do. They were recognized by church leaders so they could bring their gift to God, expecting it to be accepted as other gifts were recognized.

What Brought Their Problems to the Surface?

There was a man in the church who owned property in Cypress. His name was Joseph, but the apostles called him Barnabas, which means "the son of exhortation." Apparently, Barnabas wasn't just a believer, he was a gifted speaker who motivated people to God. Barnabas owned a plot of ground on Cypress, which was his home. *"Having land, [he] sold it, and brought the money and laid it at the apostles' feet"* (Acts 4:37), Barnabas didn't have to give the money to God but apparently was moved to do this.

Perhaps his family lineage tells the story. He was a Levite and priest who came from the Levitical family. Levites were not to own property according to the Old Testament Law (see Deut. 18:1). Somehow Barnabas had gotten away from the Lord's requirement, and he ended up owning property. When he became saved, he immediately gave his life to the Lord and began preaching to others. When God convicted him of his breaking the Old Testament Law, he did something he no longer had to do—he sold all his ground and gave it to the Lord. Since he no longer was going to be a priest and was no longer under the Old Testament Law, many think he didn't need to make the sacrifice he did. But he sold it and gave it all to God. Notice that Barnabas didn't give his money away to become a leader, but he was a leader who gave his money away. Ananias and Sapphira did the opposite. Apparently they gave away their money in the hopes of getting recognition and a place of leadership in the church.

> *What does God want from you before you give Him your money? Read Second Corinthians 8:5 for the answer.*

_____

_____

_____

_____

What Were the Inward Problems of Ananias and Sapphira?

They were guilty of deception. They were seeking the same recognition that Barnabas got. Apparently, they were envious of his leadership position, so they thought they could purchase spiritual advancement with a gift to the church.

According to Acts 5:1-2, what did they do?

_____

_____

_____

_____

They were smart enough not to directly tie their money to a request for a position. They just implied what they wanted with their timing and the amount. They wanted praise.

What does Second Corinthians 9:7 say our attitudes should be about giving?

_____

_____

_____

_____

The "praise" problem of Ananias and Sapphira was evidence of another problem: They put their confidence in their finances. They probably had this problem before they became members of the church. They worked hard for their money because it meant much to them. Because money was their security, they thought by giving what was precious to them they could get something precious in return. But believers shouldn't put their confidence in money, nor use it to get the things they want. Biblical stewardship means properly using your time, talent, and treasures for the glory of God.

According to Luke 16:11, why is the proper handling of money important to God?

_____

_____

_____

_____

What Were Their Outward Problems?

Ananias and Sapphira agreed together to deceive the church. They kept back part of the money and brought the rest to the church to get the same recognition that Barnabas got. They may have even given the same amount of money as Barnabas. But however much they gave, they suggested that their gift was the entire amount that they received from their possession.

What does Matthew 25:26 say about people who mishandle their money?

_____

_____

_____

_____

It's sad that Ananias and Sapphira collaborated to lie. The Bible says, *"his wife, also being aware of it."* This was a cold, calculated plan to deceive everyone in the church. Did they think they could deceive God? He who knows all things would not let this transgression slip by without judgment.

How Did Peter Know They Were Deceiving the Church?

The Bible doesn't tell us exactly how Peter found out that Ananias and Sapphira lied. There were several ways he could have found out. Perhaps someone in the church knew about the sale and the amount of money they received, and they told Peter. Humanly speaking, it's hard to hide sin. Divinely speaking, it's impossible.

Or perhaps no one told Peter. The Spirit of God could have spoken to him, supernaturally. Or the Spirit of God could have given Peter an inward communication.

In John 16:13, what did Jesus promise?

Ananias and Sapphira didn't say they were giving it all to God, but they let everyone think they did.

So Peter may have just known that Ananias was lying. Maybe when Ananias made a big show of giving his money, the Spirit of God whispered in Peter's ear. We'll never know how Peter learned, but we do know that he understood what was happening.

How Did Peter Sort Through a Complicated Problem?

This was a problem that could have passed unnoticed. However, because Peter found out, he had to sort through the sordid affair. First, Ananias and Sapphira didn't have to sell their property (Acts 5:4). It was theirs and God honors the ownership of property. Second, they didn't have to give all their money to the church (Acts 5:4). God had required a tithe (10 percent) in the Old Testament, and they could have given that or more if they wished.

Why should we give tithes or money gifts to God? See Malachi 3:10 and Proverbs 3:9-10 for the answer.

_____

_____

_____

_____

Third, they were obliged to tell the truth. One of the Ten Commandments instructs us not to lie, but Ananias and Sapphira ignored God's command. They were obliged to tell the truth because they were giving to the Lord Jesus who said, *"I am the Truth"* (John 14:6). In the fourth place, they had agreed to lie. Peter knew because he said, *"You have not lied to men but to God"* (Acts 5:4). He didn't accuse them of being selfish in keeping part of the money, nor did he commend them for giving as much as they did. He accused them of greed because they had agreed to lie. They wanted recognition, and they got it—but not the kind they wanted.

Why Did God Judge Them Instantaneously?

God doesn't seem to judge sin instantaneously today. If He did, there would be a lot of funerals in our churches. But for this sin, God immediately struck a couple dead. Why?

If they had gotten away with their deception, they would have corrupted the church's foundation. This happened during the beginning days of the church, and God wants His church to be holy. The Jerusalem church was going to be an example for all other churches. If the Jerusalem church got away with lying, all other churches would have been hurt. The positive influence would have been diluted, and God's work in history might not have been as effective as it's been.

Second, God demonstrated how He feels about hypocrisy. The sin of pride is one of the most grievous sins to God, so much so that he struck a couple dead who lied to Him. *"These six things the Lord hates, yes, seven are an abomination to Him: a proud look, a lying tongue…"* (Prov. 6:16-17). Notice that Ananias and Sapphira were guilty of the first two things on this continuing list.

There is a third reason why God struck them dead. Their deceit could have destroyed the soul-winning thrust of the church, but after God purged the church, soul-winning continued more effectively. After their death became known, *"believers were increasingly added to the Lord, multitudes"* (Acts 5:14). Evangelism became more effective after they were judged.

But there's a fourth reason as well. Their death brought about respect among the unsaved for the work of God. When Ananias and Sapphira were killed, it didn't hurt the church of God but rather helped it. Instead of laughing at the church, people came to the church to be saved: *"The people esteemed them highly...so that they brought the sick"* (Acts 5:13,15).

Why Did They Bury Ananias Immediately?

Instantly, young men bound the body of Ananias in cloth, took him out, and buried him. Why? First of all, the Jews did not embalm a body because they were prohibited from touching blood. Also, because of the stench, the Jews buried immediately; and to this day, many Jews bury within 24 hours of death.

But there may be a third reason why he was buried immediately. The body was considered unclean. Because Ananias was judged by God, he was unclean, and all who touched him would be unclean. In Joshua 7, Achan had sinned against God and brought reproach to Israel. He was stoned and buried immediately by the stones that were used as instruments of execution.

Why Did Peter Carefully Question Sapphira?

After Ananias was judged and buried, Sapphira came into the church about three hours later. When she entered the church, Peter did not accuse her of being in collusion, nor did he accuse her of being a co-conspirator. But rather, he asked her some careful questions: *"Tell me whether you sold the land for so much?"* (Acts 5:8). When she answered the same as her husband, Peter then made an accusation with a question, *"How is it that you have agreed together to test the Spirit of the Lord?"* (Acts 5:9).

How Did God Deal With the Couple's Deception?

Ananias and Sapphira had agreed together to deceive the church and the Lord. As a result, Sapphira also suffered. *"Then immediately she fell down at his feet and breathed her last"* (Acts 5:10). Notice the word *immediately*. This suggests how we should deal with any sin in our lives today. We should deal with our sin *immediately* because that's what God does.

Ananias and Sapphira probably wanted to bless the church by giving it some money. But God isn't glorified when we do something for Him with the wrong motive. God is not glorified when we do the *right* thing in the *wrong* way. God is glorified when you judge sin in your life. Therefore, Ananias and Sapphira brought a backhanded blessing to the church, not by the money they gave but by the judgment they suffered—*"So great fear came upon all the church and upon all who heard these things"* (Acts 5:11).

How Did Ananias and Sapphira Relate to Each Other?

First, they worked together, which could be admirable because a couple should be one in all things. But they worked together for an evil purpose. The Bible says of a couple, *"They shall become one flesh"* (Gen. 2:24), and Ananias and Sapphira probably worked well together to earn the money, but they also worked together for evil. Peter noted that they, *"Agreed together to test the Spirit of the Lord"* (Acts 5:9).

What Kind of Relationship Did They Have with Each Other?

They seemed to work as one, but to them, outward appearances were more important than inward character. They wanted to make a good impression on the church. They wanted the praise of men. They apparently did a good job hiding their desires of the flesh. Their lust for money made them sin, but apparently up until their judgment, no one in the church knew of their problem.

How could Ananias and Sapphira excuse their dishonesty? In relationship to each other, they apparently did not condemn one another nor correct one another.

They overlooked one another's dishonesty. The story might have ended differently if they had been honest with God to correct one another. But their dishonesty with the church reflected their corrupt inner character.

When couples don't truthfully relate to life, how do they keep tabs on each other? They know the other lies. When a couple catches one another lying and they don't deal with it honestly, what will eventually happen to them? First, each one will want to be the boss; they haven't learned the biblical exhortation, "Submitting yourselves one to another in the Lord." Second, both will want to get everything out of the marriage, and neither will want to give to the other. In the third place, they will keep track on how much the other has. Since possessions were important to Ananias and Sapphira, they probably kept track of the money each other had and what they each spent.

God reveals the sin we try to hide. God covers the sin from which we confess and repent.

When a husband and wife keep track of one another's money, they probably are pointing out one another's faults. When a husband and wife constantly tell one another their weaknesses, criticism becomes the glue that holds their marriage relationship together. And the glue of criticism isn't very adhesive. Rather then trying to get better, the couple will try to get even. However, true love wants the other person to always look good. When couples build up one another, they aren't looking for things to criticize, they're looking for things to praise.

Practical Take-Aways

The deception of hypocrisy.

We can be self-blinded when we make a deliberate and calculated effort to deceive others. Why? Because *"the god of this age has blinded"* (2 Cor. 4:3). What we think is all right in our sight may be a terrible sin in God's sight.

We should all recognize our inner potential to sin.

"For I know that in me (that is, in my flesh) nothing good dwells; for to will is present with me, but how to perform what is good I do not find" (Rom. 7:18). Satan is a liar. He will lie to you about what's right and he will lie to you about what's wrong. Your only basis for a correct understanding of truth is the Word of God.

If we are honest with God in all things, we can't be anything but honest with each other.

Because we are honest with God and with each other, we will be honest with the church and the world. Couples should talk about what is going on inside of them, so that their outward actions are consistent with their inner feelings. Talking has always been a path to a stable marriage.

Money can destroy a marriage.

What do most couples usually fight about? Money! Remember, money is just a symbol of your life's worth. Since you give the best of your life to earn money, you should realize that the way you treat your money is a reflection of the way you treat

friends don't keep score against friends.

life. If you lust over money and prize it more than anything else—even your marriage—then your life is all about money and the things it can buy.

How you use your money will determine how you bond your marriage together.

Because money is important, the correct use of money reflects the correct use of your life and the proper way to invest it in your marriage. In the final analysis, the correct use of money is one of the best indications of a solid marriage.

Journaling

Writing your thoughts is a discipline that makes you think clearly about a subject. Since you are serious about developing a strong marriage, use the following questions to guide your thoughts and writings. Remember, writing will clarify your thinking when you write the things you plan to do.

Example:

Lord, help us to not judge too hastily. Sometimes when getting the tithe check ready, we've thought selfishly of what we could do with that money. But we remember this account of Ananias and Sapphira and also the verses in Malachi about robbing God—"Will a man rob God? Yet you have robbed Me! But you say, 'In what way have we robbed You? In tithes and offerings'" (Mal. 3:8). Why is it, Lord, that even though we know "God loves a cheerful giver," we seem to have such a hard time tithing?

Sometimes we think we would rather give to a worthy cause than to tithe to You. Help us to give Your money back to You—willingly and cheerfully!

1. List some of the greatest things you've done for God with your money. How did you feel? Why?

His Response   *Her Response*

_____   _____

_____   _____

_____   _____

_____   _____

_____   _____

_____   _____

2. What great thing would you like to buy or build for God or His cause? A Bible college building? Distributing Sunday school literature to another culture? Paying for translating the Bible into the last remaining languages to hear about Jesus?

His Response   *Her Response*

_____   _____

_____   _____

_____   _____

_____   _____

_____   _____

3. Describe your feelings about how people give money in your church. Why do you feel that way?

His Response   *Her Response*

_____   _____

_____   _____

_____   _____

_____   _____

_____   _____

Marriage-Strengthening Exercises

Make out a family budget.

Put the tithe first because the Lord said, *"Honor the Lord with your possessions, and with the firstfruits of all your increase; so your barns will be filled with plenty, and your vats will overflow with new wine"* (Prov. 3:9-10).

Money-Spending Priorities

1. Tithes and offerings

2. Housing and utilities

3. Food

4. Clothing

5. Transportation

6. Insurance

7. Education and improvement

8. Retirement

9. Recreation

10. Entertainment

Visit a financial planner/counselor.

Some are paid, while others will help on a volunteer basis. Have them analyze your budget and spending habits. You don't have to do all they suggest, but hear from them. Make sure to communicate to the financial planner your spiritual priorities. It's good to articulate your financial dream to someone outside the family.

Chapter 12

Abraham and Sarah
LEARNING TO LIVE WITH PROBLEMS

Introduction by David and Cathy Earley
New Life Church, Gahanna, Ohio

Some people accomplish their greatest work for God in the second half of life. We are delighted to introduce this chapter because we feel our greatest ministry is in front of us—like Abraham and Sarah—even though we have already served the Lord 21 years in both church and community ministries.

Abraham and Sarah were middle-aged when they left Ur of the Chaldees and headed for the Promised Land. God taught them many lessons as they lived in tents in various locations. God's promise was that Abraham and Sarah would have a son, and through that son the Messiah, Jesus Christ, would bless the entire world.

Abraham and Sarah followed their human instincts on several occasions, attempting to thwart the will of God. But their experience in the Promised Land is the experience of many people in life today. People attempt to thwart the will of God by doing foolish things.

But faith made the difference. Despite his age, Abraham, *"not being weak in faith…did not consider his own body, already dead (since he was about a hundred years old), and the deadness of Sarah's womb. He did not waver at the promise of God through unbelief, but was strengthened in faith, giving glory to God, and being fully convinced that what He had promised He was also able to perform"* (Rom. 4:19-21).

And what was Abraham and Sarah's greatest achievement? Both the birth and the raising of Isaac to be a godly young man who would carry on the promised seed through whom the Messiah would come. We hope that our greatest personal achievement will be the raising of three boys to be godly young men.

Therefore, let all of you who are in the second half of life take comfort as you study this chapter. God can still use you—not to have children—but to have spiritual children, to do your greatest work for God, to accomplish more in the twilight of your life than you did in the beginning of your life. That's faith—that's hope—that's our challenge.

Learning to Live With Problems

Hebrews 11:8-19

When a man and woman marry, they pledge their lives to each other, "Till death do us part." When they are young, neither thinks about the death of the other. They still have strong bodies, and their present lives are so good that death is far removed from their thoughts. Abraham and Sarah had lifelong struggles with "life problems" until they died. God promised a son—a new life. But Sarah couldn't have children because she was barren. They tried to fulfill the promise their own way by using a maid-servant and only brought grief to themselves.

Finally, when they trusted God, Isaac was born. Abraham and Sarah lived by faith, but they also had some problems and failures. Their lives are examples to us. Even when Sarah died, Abraham showed us how to deal with the death of a spouse with strength and dignity.

What Are the Two Greatest Attributes Mentioned about Sarah in the New Testament?

Faith was Sarah's greatest quality. She was listed in Hebrews 11, God's Hall of Fame, even though she seemed to have momentary lapses in judgment. Sarah's second greatest quality was her obedience to Abraham—*"as Sarah obeyed Abraham"* (1 Pet. 3:6). In this act, she fulfilled Paul's expectation of marriage, *"Submitting to one another in the fear of God. Wives, submit to your own husbands, as to the Lord"* (Eph. 5:21-22). Notice the New Testament word is *submit* which means an internal decision. Some have mistakenly quoted this verse using the word *subject,* which implies another person's effort to press the wife into submission.

It's important to clarify this concept of submission. Men and women alike have been offended by the notion that this phrase means the wife is under absolute control of her husband. That is not accurate. In a marriage, husbands and wives do have very different roles. The husband is charged with caring for his wife the way Christ loved the church (see Eph. 5:25). Her "submission" is a completely voluntary act that merely means she recognizes and respects his leadership role in the family. In fact, Ephesians 5:21 clearly states that couples should be "submitting to one another." This refers to how *all* Christian people should relate to one another.

The beauty of submission is that the door handle is on the *inside*, and a wife voluntarily submits to her husband as unto the Lord. What best encourages her to do that? She will submit voluntarily to her husband when he leads her as Christ leads the Church.

In Hebrews 11:11, Sarah's incredible faith was rewarded. What did she receive?

How Difficult Was It for Sarah to Submit to Abraham?

Sometimes it can be a difficult and costly transition for a woman to leave her family and take up residence with a new husband. Notice what God told Abraham to do: *"Get out of your country, from your family and from your father's house"* (Gen. 12:1). But Sarah followed her husband. She left her family and friends just as Abraham left his in Ur of the Chaldees to go to the land of Israel. Of all the things Sarah did for God, this might have been one of the most difficult. But sacrifice has always been part of following the Lord: *"If anyone desires to come after Me, let him deny himself, and take up his cross daily, and follow Me"* (Luke 9:23).

Abraham left his home without a map, and he didn't know where he was going (see Heb. 11:8). Women generally prefer security over surprises. They like their homes to be settled and their family relationships secure. So great faith was certainly visible in Sarah's willingness to follow Abraham when he didn't even know where they were going.

What Do We Know About Sarah's Character?

Sarah's name means "princess," which describes her beauty, culture, education, charm, and gracious manner of life. From all that we can determine, Sarah walked through the camp with grace and dignity. What better way to describe the woman of God than to say she has dignity. Sarah was admired for her faithful life by those who lived around her. She is admired by New Testament believers who read about her today.

The focus of Sarah's life was to be a helpmeet to her husband, just as God originally described Eve as a helpmeet to Adam.

According to Genesis 2:18, why did God give Adam a helpmeet and how did the helpmeet compare to him?

_____

_____

_____

_____

Sarah became a "helper comparable" to Abraham because when she made a conscious decision to follow her husband and help him fulfill God's plan for his life, she epitomized the true helpmeet.

Note that a helpmeet was definitely not weak. At times Sarah questioned Abraham's decisions, and at other times she had a strong opinion about what they should do. When a husband has a helpmeet, he has someone who will seek to meet his needs just as he meets hers. A helpmeet will help him through difficult times—aiding him to make decisions he can't make, and helping him learn things he doesn't know.

In your weakness you discover strength. In your strength you help the other become strong.

Sarah was a wonderful helpmeet. Wherever Abraham went, Sarah went. And whatever Abraham did, Sarah was a valuable part of that. Some wives may interfere with God's plan for their lives by not following the Lord in helping their husband.

Sarah once interfered with God's plan by taking matters into her own hands. This placed a great strain on her marriage to Abraham. God had promised they would have a child, and through this child would come a great nation. Ultimately this child would lead to the Messiah. But the problem was that they had no child. They were old and every year that they got older, having a child seemed less likely. In those days, being barren was dishonoring, and Sarah was past the age of bearing children. It seemed futile to hope against nature.

What does Genesis 16:2 say Sarah did?

_____

_____

_____

_____

What Was the Nature of Sarah's Unwise Solution?

A couple of conclusions can be drawn from Sarah's decision. First, it should be recognized that she was following a legal transaction of her culture. The Nuzi customs of that day provided for obtaining a legal child by a bond slave. But the most obvious issue about this time in Sarah's life was her uncharacteristic lack of faith. God had promised that Abraham would have a son. While the promise did not include her, it surely implied her. For some reason, Sarah put herself outside that promise. She didn't believe that God could bring life from a dead womb, or that God could give a son to an aged couple. So Sarah made a decision she thought was the right one.

Why does God allow problems in our lives? And what will trouble do for you?
Go to James 1:2 for the answer.

_____

_____

_____

_____

The young maid Hagar got pregnant by Abraham just as Sarah suggested. Then problems broke out around the camp. Hagar became demanding, eventually wanting to be treated equally to Sarah. Though Hagar was still a slave, she may have even wanted to replace Sarah.

Sarah blamed Abraham when Hagar became unmanageable. Communication is usually better than isolation, but this was communication with a hook. Abraham responded by doing nothing about the problem. The Scriptures are silent as to whether Abraham talked with Hagar or whether he made concessions. Sometimes men are emotionally unable or unwilling to act when problems face the family. But when problems are not dealt with wisely and faithfully, they tend to grow. Even if unresolved problems subside for a time, they eventually return with greater impact.

According to James 1:5, what should you do when you're in trouble?

_____

_____

Abraham didn't assume family leadership, as he should have. And leadership is what most women expect from their husbands. Abraham didn't act or provide leadership, and in the final analysis, he neglected his responsibility to his wife, to Hagar, and to God.

Ultimately, Hagar departed from the camp, but only for a short period of time. When God saw her pain, He sent her back with the promise that she would bear a son, and that he would be a great nation. And just as God told her, Hagar had a son—Ishmael.

Years later, little Isaac was born to Sarah and Abraham. This was a miracle by our standards today! They were both well past what we would consider childbearing age.

> *You have already made a decision when you refuse to choose; you've made a decision about the things you'll lose.*

The name *Isaac* means "laughter," and it was given because both Abraham and Sarah laughed at the prospect of the birth of a son. God told Abraham to call the child "Laughter" as a pleasant reminder of His challenge to their faith.

Somewhere between the time of Sarah's laughter of unbelief and the birth of the son, her laughter turned to joy, and her joy turned to belief.

In Genesis 21:6, what did Sarah say God did?

_____

_____

_____

_____

And in First Peter 1:7, how does it say we should relate to the Lord after He has helped us through problems?

_____

_____

_____

_____

What Brought About Another Disagreement between Sarah and Abraham?

When little Isaac was about three years old, the time came for him to be weaned. This seems strange to us today, especially in an age of premixed formula and all of our advanced child-rearing techniques. But in desert tribes of Bible times, a child wasn't weaned until age three, and sometimes even later!

Abraham planned a great banquet for the occasion. During the banquet, Hagar and Ishmael, who was about 13 years old by this time, began mocking little Isaac. The Hebrew word for *mock* indicates they were striking him with their hands or fists.

Sarah was rightfully upset at what Hagar and Ishmael were doing.

In Genesis 21:10, what does Sarah tell Abraham to do?

_____

_____

_____

_____

Abraham's inability to assure Sarah and preserve peace again threatened to drive a wedge between them. The sins of a father can easily reemerge in the life of his son, and that was the case with Isaac. He chose one son, Esau, while his wife, Rebekah, chose the other son, Jacob. And it didn't stop there. Jacob drove a wedge in his family because he loved Joseph more than his other sons, while Leah seemed to favor Judah.

There are many instances in the Bible of people with troubles. In Job 5:7, for instance, who has problems in their lives?

_____

_____

_____

_____

What Is a Wife's Role in Problem Solving?

The Bible says that Sarah was "submissive" to Abraham, yet at times she astutely pointed out the other side of an issue to him. She had her opinion while Abraham had his opinion, but the Bible still says *"Sarah obeyed Abraham"* (1 Pet. 3:6). Even in a healthy submission, a wife should have *strong opinions* about problems, and she must *share* in the responsibility for resolving them.

According to James 1:2, what should be your attitude when you go through troubles?

_____

_____

_____

Now look in Ephesians 4:22-24. What should you do to overcome your problems and trials?

_____

_____

_____

_____

What about the wife who always gives in to her husband? Is this healthy? The wife who loves peace at any cost and who avoids responsibility may have some esteem issues. She needs to see herself in God's sight as a woman called, commissioned, and responsible to give her family the best of her wisdom and love. Just as the husband provides leadership to the family, the wife often becomes the glue that holds them all together.

When One Mate Dies First

We said earlier, when a man and woman marry, they marry "til death do us part." Abraham and Sarah had a long and profitable marriage. But when she reached the age of 123, *"Sarah died"* (Gen. 23:2). Death is inevitable…it comes to all. In this family, the wife died first. Interestingly, Sarah is the only woman in the Bible whose age is mentioned, and only after she was dead. Whether intended or not, fellas, this may be a wise example for all of us of the sensitivity to a woman's privacy about her age.

What Was Abraham's Emotional Response to the Death of His Wife?

Obviously, when someone has become a part of your life and he or she dies, a part of you dies. It is because in marriage, two people become one flesh, and when one dies, suddenly the remaining one feels very incomplete. Half of Abraham's life was gone, half of his stability was gone, and half of his reason for living was gone.

First, Genesis 23:2 says Abraham mourned over Sarah. This is the inward grief that he felt over her loss. There may not be tears or outward emotions, but there is grief as deep as their relationship. In the same verse, however, it does say that Abraham "wept" for Sarah. For some time, Abraham must have felt great loneliness. When he went to talk to the leaders in Hebron to ask for a place to bury Sarah, he said, *"I am a foreigner and a visitor among you"* (Gen. 23:4). He no doubt felt alone because his helpmeet was gone.

In the face of death, you can't rest on your past; you must face the future, even though it may be a difficult one. There may be a long time of mourning, and the ache of loneliness for one's mate may never go away completely.

A Man Is Wise to Listen to His Wife...

1. When she says there is a problem in the marriage.

2. When she has an evaluation.

3. When she expresses her needs and feelings.

4. When she expresses a desire for certain changes.

What does Genesis 23:3 say Abraham did after he mourned the death of his wife?

_____

_____

_____

_____

_____

_____

This means Abraham stood up, gathered himself, and got on with his life. If you should experience the loss of your mate, you must eventually look to the future because God's plan is for you to live in the future. You can't remain in the past.

Go to James 1:12 to find out what reward is promised to those who successfully endure troubles and trials.

_____

_____

_____

_____

Practical Take-Aways

The submission of a wife is not a posture of surrender but an attitude of trust.

At the beginning, Sarah was willing to follow Abraham anywhere. She was willingly submissive, but that doesn't mean she was dominated. She had strong opinions. Sometimes she was right, sometimes she was wrong. But so was her husband. Their submission to each other was a lifelong journey. At times, Abraham made it easy, especially when he served God. At other times, Abraham made it difficult when he followed his flesh.

There's no such thing as a life of faith without problems.

God doesn't measure your faith by the absence of problems. Your faith is evidenced when it empowers you to face and overcome problems. Abraham is described as "walking by faith," yet he had problems with the economy, relatives, his wife, fleshly desires, and evil, warring neighbors. You can be in the center of God's will if you have problems, but you continue to follow God by facing problems and overcoming them with godly wisdom and faith.

How we handle problems will influence our children.

We may or may not like it, but our children are often more like us than we ever know. Even if they try not to, our kids can pick up our bad habits. If we remain aware of this, we can work to overcome our bad habits and give our kids a good example. Nevertheless, because our kids will repeatedly witness that we are sinners, a life of repentance and dependence on God's strength will be our most valuable example to them. Then we talk with our kids and try to point them in the right direction.

Our days are known.

In virtually all marriages, one spouse must eventually say goodbye to the other. The important thing is not what death takes from you, even though it feels that you've lost part of yourself. The important thing is how you go forward from your loss. You will mourn and grieve, to be sure. But at some point, you'll need to leave the cemetery. God intends your life with Him to continue prospering.

Journaling

Writing your thoughts is a good habit that will help you think clearly about a subject. Since you are serious about developing a strong marriage, you can use the following questions to guide your thoughts and writings. Remember, writing your prayers and plans will clarify your thinking.

For example:

Lord, there are so many examples in the lives of Abraham and Sarah that are true for all of us. Sometimes we're moved away from family and we miss them. Sometimes we tend to play favorites with our children. Sometimes our faith isn't very strong. Help us remember that You have never failed and that when problems come, we can face them together. Lord, you have blessed our lives individually and together. Help me to carefully think through my suggestions to my spouse. I never want to misdirect him or her. Help us both to ask You for wisdom in all our decisions. Amen.

1. Write in your own words how you feel when God answers your prayers and solves a problem.

His Response   *Her Response*

_____   _____

_____   _____

_____   _____

_____   _____

2. Make a list of the three greatest problems God has solved in your marriage. How did you feel? How did you express your gratitude to God? Did it bring the two of you closer together? Did it strengthen your faith?

His Response   *Her Response*

_____   _____

_____   _____

_____   _____

_____   _____

3. What have you learned about your mate by the way he or she solves a problem? How can you help your mate? What can you learn from your mate?

His Response

Her Response

_____   _____

_____   _____

_____   _____

_____   _____

4. What have you learned about God from the way your mate solves problems? Write what helped you in the past that can also help you in the future.

His Response

Her Response

_____   _____

_____   _____

_____   _____

_____   _____

Marriage-Strengthening Exercises

Keep a journal.

Keep a separate journal in which you record details about needs, problems, or any prayer that you need answered. Pray about them individually, and then pray for them together. As God answers your prayers, check them off (I write "Amen") and describe the resolution. Keep the journal for future reference and encouragement. Sometime in the future, when you think God can't answer (or you think He's not listening), take out your past answers to prayer and review them. (My pages date back to 1951!)

Plan a conference.

Plan a conference with your mate to discuss your strategy to handle problems. Brainstorm! Make a list of the greatest challenges you have faced victoriously in your marriage. Begin writing your principles of handling problems, and then make a list of past problems that went unresolved. Discuss ways you might have approached the problems differently. Be careful to avoid accusing one another. Continue writing the principles that worked to solve problems. Add to your list the principles that were not effective in your marriage. When you finish this conference, you should have a better handle on solving future problems.

How to Solve a Problem God's Way

1. Get the facts.

2. Pray about it.

3. Establish needed biblical principles.

4. Pray that God will give you guidance.

5. Write out the problem and clarify it.

6. Ask God for wisdom.

7. Make a list of various ways to solve the problem.

8. Ask God to help you make good choices.

9. Choose the best solution.

10. Implement the solution the best way possible.

11. Pray for continued strength and wisdom, and thank God for His grace and leadership in your life.

Conclusion

Elmer and I hope you enjoyed reading about these 12 biblical couples. There is much to learn from each of them. We still enjoy reading about the people God has used and those He continues to use to further His Kingdom on earth.

Whether you've been recently married or have recently celebrated a decade or two of marriage, keeping Christ at the center of your lives will assure you a lifetime of happily ever afters!

About the Authors

Ruth & Elmer L. Towns

Elmer L. Towns, co-founder of Liberty University, a college and seminary professor, dean of the School of Religion, is also the author of numerous popular and scholarly works. He is a Gold Medallion Award-winning author whose books include *Fasting for Spiritual Breakthrough* and the *Praying the Scriptures* series, which includes 13 best-selling books. Ruth Towns is an active member of her church and retired director of an adoption agency. She teaches at Liberty University, Lynchburg, Virginia, and is the author of *Women Gifted for Ministry*. The Towns' have been married for more than 57 years.

Authors' Note

Ruth and I found two books that were helpful when we began research for this book. *Famous Couples in the Bible* by Richard Strauss was a valuable resource for us. We are grateful for the ideas it provided and give credit to its influence on our book. This was an exciting find because Richard and his wife, Mary, were our friends at Dallas Theological Seminary from 1954 to 1958.

The second book we found was *The Way of a Man with a Maid* by Clarence Edward McCartney. It is an enjoyable collection of sermons on Bible couples.

About the Contributors

Tim and Beverly LaHaye

Noted author, minister, educator, and nationally recognized speaker Dr. Tim LaHaye has authored more than 50 books on Bible prophecy. His fiction series, *Left Behind*, coauthored with Jerry Jenkins, is the all-time best-selling Christian fiction series. Tim is also the president of Tim LaHaye Ministries and cofounder of the Pre-Trib Research Center. Beverly LaHaye is a nationally recognized advocate and spokeswoman on issues affecting women and the family, and is the founder and chairperson of Concerned Women of America. She is also the author of many books including several she co-wrote with her husband, Tim. The LaHaye's have been married for 62 years. They wrote the Foreword of this book.

Pastor David Yonggi and Grace Kim-Cho

Author and speaker Dr. David Yonggi Cho was the senior pastor (now retired) of The Yoido Full Gospel Church in Seoul, Korea, the largest church in the world with more than 830,000 members. He is the author of more than 100 books and the recipient of a Gold Medallion Award. Dr. Cho's wife, Grace Kim-Cho, is an accomplished composer and pianist. The Cho's have three grown sons and have been married for over 44 years. They wrote the introduction to Isaac and Rebekah.

Mike and Cindy Jacobs

Mike Jacobs, a former business analyst, has been commissioned by God to bring unity and order to the Body of Christ. A key focus of Mike's vision is teaching on

Christ's transforming power in the business world, governmental structures, the church, and the community at large. Widely recognized as a prophet to the nations, Dr. Cindy Jacobs is the president and co-founder of Generals International, a missionary organization devoted to training in prayer and spiritual warfare. She is the author of three best-selling books, including *Possessing the Gates of the Enemy*, *The Voice of God*, and *Women of Destiny*. The Jacobs' have been married for 36 years. They wrote the introduction to Jacob and Rachel.

Bill and Vonette Bright

Dr. Bill Bright, along with his wife, Vonette, founded Campus Crusade for Christ. Before his death in 2003, he authored more than 100 books, as well as thousands of articles and pamphlets that have been distributed in many languages throughout the world. The Brights received numerous awards for their work over the years, including a Lifetime Achievement Award from both the National Association of Evangelicals and the Evangelical Christian Publishers Association. Vonette Bright's commitment to prayer led to the founding of the National Prayer Committee. She has authored *My Heart in His Hands*, a devotional series, and co-authored *The Joy of Hospitality*. The Bright's had been married for 54 years. They wrote the introduction to Adam and Eve.

John and Margaret Maxwell

Speaker and author Dr. John C. Maxwell is a gifted authority on leadership and mentor to thousands. Dr. Maxwell established INJOY Group and EQUIP ministries, and has authored more than 30 books, including such *New York Times* best-sellers as *Failing Forward* and *The 21 Irrefutable Laws of Leadership*. His work continues to shape and accelerate the careers of business people around the world. Margaret Maxwell has been John's helpmeet, best friend, and most ardent supporter. They have been married for 40 years. They wrote the introduction to Aquila and Priscilla.

Ed and Donna Hindson

Dr. Ed Hindson is the president of World Prophetic Ministry. He is also a Bible teacher on "The King Is Coming" telecast, and the Assistant Chancellor and Dean of the Tim LaHaye School of Prophecy Institute of Biblical Studies at Liberty University in Virginia. Dr. Hindson and his wife, Donna, have been married for 43 years and have three children and five grandchildren. They wrote the introduction to Xerxes and Esther.

Tim and Julie Clinton

Tim Clinton is the author of *Before a Bad Goodbye: How to Turn Your Marriage Around* and *The Marriage You've Always Wanted.* He is both a professional counselor and a marriage and family therapist, is the current president of the nearly 50,000-member American Association of Christian Counselors (AACC), he is Professor of Counseling and pastoral care, and Executive Director of the Center for Counseling and Family Studies at Liberty University. Tim and his wife, Julie, reside with their children in Lynchburg, Virginia. They wrote the introduction to Samson and Delilah.

Ed and Jo Beth Young

Dr. Ed Young is the pastor of Second Baptist Church in Houston, Texas, and founder of the broadcast ministry, "The Winning Walk," which is seen and heard across North America. He is the author of *Against All Odds, Romancing the Home, Pure Sex,* and *Everywhere I Go.* Jo Beth Young is very active in her church, leading many adult Bible studies. She is also an eloquent speaker for seminars and women's retreats. The Young's have been married for 50 years. They wrote the introduction to David and Bathsheba.

John Ed and Lynn Mathison

Dr. John Ed Mathison has retired as the senior minister of Frazer Memorial United Methodist Church in Montgomery, Alabama, after serving for 36 years. He is a nationally known and sought-after speaker, particularly at the Billy Graham Training Center at The Cove. He has written five books, *Tried and True, Every Member in Ministry, Fishing for Birds, Extra Effort,* and *Treasures of the Transformed Life.* He also writes for *Decision* magazine, *The Circuit Rider,* and other religious periodicals. Lynn Mathison, an interior decorator, has provided leadership to the women's ministry at Frazer church and is also a speaker for women's retreats and seminars. The Mathison's have been married for 13 years. They wrote the introduction to Boaz and Ruth.

Jerry and Macel Falwell

Jerry Falwell was the founding pastor of Lynchburg's Thomas Road Baptist Church, and served there as the senior pastor for over 50 years. Thirty-eight years ago, he also founded Liberty University and continued to serve as the Chancellor until his death in 2007. He authored over 18 books and conducted a weekly international television program. Macel Falwell is an artist and pianist. She had served as the Thomas Road Baptist Church pianist since the founding of the congregation in 1956. She enrolled in college at the age of 50 and later became an English instructor at Liberty University. Jerry would often say, "Macel is my best critic and is most responsible for the successful lives and careers of our children and myself." The Falwell's had been married for 49 years. They wrote the introduction to Joseph and Mary.

D. James and Anne Kennedy

Dr. D. James Kennedy was the pastor of Coral Ridge Presbyterian Church, one of the largest Presbyterian churches in America, until his death in 2007. His energetic commitment to both evangelism and cultural renewal is demonstrated by four organizations he founded: Evangelism Explosion International, Knox Theological

Seminary, Coral Ridge Ministries Media, Inc., and Westminster Academy. Dr. Kennedy and his wife, Anne, wrote the introduction to Zechariah and Elizabeth.

Neil T. and Joanne Anderson

Dr. Neil T. Anderson is the founder of Freedom in Christ Ministries. He has nearly 25 years of pastoral experience and has taught for more than 10 years at seminary and post-graduate levels. Neil has authored many best-selling books on spiritual freedom. Joanne Anderson has been an integral part of her husband's various ministries. The Anderson's have two children and two grandchildren, and have been married for over 42 years. They wrote the introduction to Ananias and Sapphira.

Dave and Cathy Earley

Dave and Cathy Earley's claims to fame are that they love God, love each other, and really enjoy their three sons: Daniel, Andrew, and Luke. Dave and Cathy started a church in their basement over 20 years ago. Dave is Chairman of the Department of Pastoral Leadership at Liberty Baptist Theological Seminary and Liberty University. He also serves as Director of the Center for Ministry Training at Liberty Baptist Theological Seminary, and the Director of the Center for Church Planting of Liberty University. Dave has written 12 books and several church health resources. Dave and Cathy spend their free time enjoying biking, hiking, and sports. The Earleys have been married for 28 years. They wrote the introduction to Abraham and Sarah.

Additional copies of this book and other book titles from DESTINY IMAGE are available at your local bookstore.

Call toll-free: 1-800-722-6774.

Send a request for a catalog to:

Destiny Image® Publishers, Inc.

P.O. Box 310
Shippensburg, PA 17257-0310

"Speaking to the Purposes of God for This Generation and for the Generations to Come."

For a complete list of our titles, visit us at www.destinyimage.com.